"Risa hits all the key points for improving self-esteem including tools for changing thought patterns, applying mindfulness, accepting compliments, overcoming perfectionism, and more. Applicable for adults and youth alike, I look forward to introducing my own emerging adolescents to this book!"

—*Erica Curtis, licensed marriage and family therapist, book author and mother of three*

"Risa Williams writes with such warmth and earnest kindness that she makes us feel empowered to improve ourselves and find our way to much less stressful lives."

—*Maggie Lynch, CEO and book author*

"This is an important and much-needed book that will empower individuals to feel better about themselves right now and I've already started implementing it with myself and my clients with tremendous results. Another fantastic book from Risa Williams!"

—*Dr Tamara Soles, psychologist, podcast host, and founder of The Secure Child Centre, Montreal*

"As a psychotherapist, I was most interested in 'The Evidence Investigator', because people often accept their thinking as fact and fail to evaluate it to see if it is logical and rational based on the evidence they have. This book teaches people how to engage in the metacognitive process, or thinking about their own thinking, which is crucial to shaping our perceptions of ourselves."

—*Stevon Lewis, licensed therapist, author, and host of* How to Talk to High Achievers About Anything

The Ultimate Self-Esteem Toolkit

25 Tools to Boost Confidence, Achieve Goals, and Find Happiness

Risa Williams

Illustrated by Jennifer Whitney

Jessica Kingsley Publishers
London and Philadelphia

First published in Great Britain in 2023 by Jessica Kingsley Publishers
An imprint of Hodder & Stoughton Ltd
An Hachette Company

1

A CIP catalogue record for this title is available from the
British Library and the Library of Congress

ISBN 978 1 83997 474 8
eISBN 978 1 83997 475 5

Printed and bound in the United States by Integrated Books International

Jessica Kingsley Publishers' policy is to use papers that are natural,
renewable, and recyclable products and made from wood grown in
sustainable forests. The logging and manufacturing processes are expected
to conform to the environmental regulations of the country of origin.

Jessica Kingsley Publishers
Carmelite House
50 Victoria Embankment
London EC4Y 0DZ

www.jkp.com

For everyone who reads this book,
I hope it helps you in some small way.

Contents

Acknowledgements

For Jane Evans who edited this book and *The Ultimate Anxiety Toolkit*, for Sean Townsend who edited *The Ultimate Time Management Toolkit*, and Hannah Snetsinger and all the wonderful people at Jessica Kingsley Publishers who worked on my last three books...

For Maggie Lynch, who told me to practice the feelings I want to feel...

For Mike Sonksen, who told me to keep writing...

For Jennifer Whitney, who illustrated this book and the last two...

For my family, who taught me to be strong...

For Zach, who taught me how to relax...

For my kids, who help me find the fun...

For all the wonderful clients, students, and colleagues I have interacted with over the years who tested out these tools and told me what worked for them...

For everyone who read my last books and wrote encouraging words online...

For Eden Byrne and Ezra Werb who helped me get through the creative process...

For David Burns, Thich Nhat Hanh, Dr Viktor Frankl, Dr Ned Hallowell, Joseph Campbell, Brené Brown, Aaron Beck, Martin Seligman, Esther Hicks, and C.S. Jung, for writing books that have uplifted so many people...

For Erica Curtis, Dulcie Yamanaka, Dr Tamara Soles, Dr Tarryn MacCarthy, Dr Michael Feldmeier, Dr Scott Waltman, Stevon Lewis, Cynthia

Siadat, Cara Dolan, Julissa Padilla, Carla King, Andrew Lawston, Trevor Stockwell, Yeukai Kajidori, Amanda Way, Solomon Carreiro, Andrew Ralles, Chiwan Choi, and all the other kind people who provided positive boosts along the way…

For all the readers out there…

Thank you.

I appreciate you!

To read more writing by Risa Williams, please visit:

www.risawilliams.com

www.theultimatetoolkitbooks.com

Listen to *The Motivation Mindset Podcast with Risa Williams* at:

https://www.risawilliams.com/motivationmindset.html

and follow her at @risawilliamstherapy

Introduction

How do you feel about yourself right now? Chances are, if you've picked up this book, it's because you want to find ways to like yourself more, to appreciate who you have become, and to learn how to be kinder to yourself on a daily basis. And that's a wonderful start, one that can lead you to many positive changes ahead.

In my last two books, *The Ultimate Anxiety Toolkit* and *The Ultimate Time Management Toolkit*, I wanted to help people navigate subjects that often feel overwhelming and difficult to manage by providing practical, easy to use tools that can be applied to everyday situations.

In the same way, with this book, I am hoping to provide simple tools that will make you realize that being kinder to yourself is entirely possible to do right here and right now.

My path to finding a healthy sense of self-esteem was pretty bumpy, to say the least. Growing up, I didn't have many examples of grown-ups with healthy self-esteem, and I spent much of my younger adult years navigating the intensely competitive worlds of ballet and the film industry feeling like I wasn't "doing enough" and that I wasn't "good enough." Somewhere during these experiences, I had accidentally created a harsh inner critic that would often chime in with negative feedback, like, "You're not moving fast enough!" or "You're messing it all up!" or "You don't know what you're doing!"

While your past experiences may differ from mine, it's also possible that you have your own type of inner critic badgering you a lot, too. We all have one; it may act and sound different, but it almost always makes us feel bad about ourselves when we listen to it for too long.

After going to graduate school for psychology, becoming a mom who really wanted her own kids to have a healthy sense of self-esteem, and then becoming a licensed therapist who was actively coaching clients to improve their confidence in stressful situations, I came to the conclusion that it was finally time for me to practice what I was preaching. It was time for me to change my own self-talk in a more positive direction for good. It was time for me to take the steering wheel back from the inner critic and to start driving myself where I really wanted to go instead.

Around this time, I discovered cognitive behavioral therapy, mindfulness, narrative therapy, and positive psychology. Using ideas from many modalities, I began to develop some self-esteem strategies that helped me connect with my own inner strength and my own sense of agency more. And then, slowly (and not without many setbacks), I started to develop kinder self-talk that was more encouraging, gentle, and soothing, more of the time.

We often feel like we can be nice, kind, encouraging, and supportive to other people, while being harsh, mean and overly critical to ourselves. Once you realize how unfair this is, and how truly distorted this idea is, you'll start to approach things differently.

Although self-esteem issues can sometimes stem from trauma, our past, the hardships we've faced, and other emotional and physical issues that may be different for each person experiencing them, it is my hope that the tools in this book will help you start to find new ways to be kinder to yourself in the present moment.

It is recommended that you seek out professional help from a doctor or therapist to address any psychological, emotional, or past issues that you may need help processing. This book is intended as a supplemental tool and not a replacement for therapy or medical advice. It is simply meant to provide new creative ideas that can hopefully help you start to shift your daily thinking habits in a more positive direction.

What I've found, both personally, and from my work with many clients and students over the years, is that feelings of self-esteem and confidence can often be improved by addressing a few factors. The tools in this book are designed to help you with these factors:

- **Changing your self-talk:** When we say motivating and gentle things to ourselves all day long, our self-esteem naturally starts to rise. Conversely, when we say critical and reprimanding things to ourselves all day long, our feelings of self-esteem tend to sink. The first tools in this book can help you to change your self-talk because, after you do, the other tools in the book will become much easier to use.

- **Your sense of agency and resiliency: Agency** comes from acknowledging that you are the one in charge of changing your thinking and fully accepting that no one else can do it for you. **Resiliency** is our sense of how effectively we handle problems that block our path, and how quickly we recover from setbacks we face. Many of the tools in this book can help you learn how to change your thinking patterns and how to ground yourself when you're faced with obstacles in everyday life.

- **Stress reduction skills:** Stress exacerbates problems that already exist in our thinking patterns. So, when you get stressed out, any intense thoughts you already have going on tend to feel even *more* intense. Learning ways to bring down your stress can help you to regulate your mental, emotional, and physical wellbeing so that you can find your calm again.

- **Balancing out "extreme thinking": Extreme thinking** is when you tend to see things in black or white categories: for example, things are perfect or a disaster, you are either loved or hated, you feel amazing or you feel terrible. Extreme thinking can also include the "maximization" of our perceived flaws and the "minimization" of our strengths, blaming and labeling ourselves, disqualifying positive feedback we receive, and frequently jumping to negative conclusions throughout everyday life. Many of the tools in this book are designed to help you start to shift away from seeing things in negative extremes in order to find your balance again. When you choose balance over extremes, you can empower yourself with perspective.

- **Connecting with your small successes more:** How often do you actually let yourself feel proud, accomplished, happy, joyful, playful, excited, or delighted? How often do you intentionally seek these types of feelings out instead of zooming in on the stress, anxiety, fear, and frustration that can be so easy for our brains to fall into? Learning to actively look for good things in your life and to actively see good things in yourself is an essential part of building healthier self-esteem. Think of it as the final boss level! And you can level up, one step at a time.

Self-esteem is how we tend to feel about ourselves, how we appreciate, soothe, and care for ourselves on a regular basis, and **confidence** is about how we feel about our ability to do certain tasks and navigate certain situations in a particular moment. While there is usually overlap between the two, sometimes, it's entirely possible to feel confident about doing a specific activity but to also feel a sense of low self-esteem overall at the same time.

However, when you learn how to deliberately shift your **self-talk** more frequently, when you strengthen your sense of **personal agency**, when you actively lean into kinder thoughts about yourself more deliberately, and when you learn to connect with the feelings you want to feel more of the time, your feelings of self-esteem will start to shift and your confidence to navigate a variety of future situations will naturally start to grow.

Start off by playing around with each idea in this book as you read it. Take time to mull things over, to journal about things, and to fill out the worksheets as they can help you custom-tailor the tools to suit your own needs.

Change doesn't have to be instant or dramatic to be effective. It can also happen in smaller, easier to manage steps, and still have a big overall impact on your life.

By taking your time with each tool in this book, it is my hope that you can get to a place where you can be kinder to yourself on a daily basis, one that allows you to feel really good about yourself more frequently.

I believe you can do it!

The question is, do you?

Let's start by practicing that feeling…one chapter at a time.

CHAPTER 1

When You Want to Change Your Thinking...

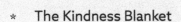

* The Kindness Blanket
* The Self-Talk Meter

* The Evidence Investigator
* The Instant Replay

THE KINDNESS BLANKET

To start off this book, here's a warm-up exercise that can help you to start to think in a much gentler way about yourself. When we have the flu or a cold, most of us instinctively know to get into bed, not move around too much, eat a little soup, sip some hot tea, watch a relaxing TV show, read a lightweight book, and basically, not really do much of anything except let our bodies reset. In other words, our bodies are telling us to go easy, and if we're listening, that's exactly what we do. We listen to our bodies. We go easy on ourselves. We give ourselves permission to rest until we feel a little better.

However, when it comes to how our brains feel, it's often quite a different story. When we've been really stressed out, or when we've spent a really long time criticizing ourselves, we may have also released some uncomfortable stress hormones into our systems, such as cortisol and adrenaline, which can make us feel really bad.

Neuroscience nugget: According to Dr Teresa Aubele and Susan Reynolds, "Negative thinking slows down brain coordination, making it difficult to process thoughts and find solutions. Feeling frightened, which often happens when focused on negative outcomes, has been shown to decrease activity in your cerebellum, which slows the brain's ability to process new information—limiting your ability to practice creative problem-solving. Additionally, the fear factor impacts your left temporal lobe, which affects mood, memory, and impulse control" (Aubele and Reynolds 2011).

When we're feeling bad emotionally, we should have the same instinct as when we feel bad physically, which is to go easy on ourselves, to take it easy, and to rest for a little while. We should really give ourselves permission to fully reset ourselves until we feel a little better.

However, what I've witnessed many people do (and what I've often done myself) is the exact opposite of this. Often, when people feel emotionally exhausted and mentally fried, instead of slowing down and treating themselves in a gentler way, they double-down on whatever it is they're doing that's making them feel bad (they work even harder, they keep pushing themselves through tasks, they keep criticizing themselves and telling themselves they're doing a bad job at whatever it is they're trying to accomplish in this stressed-out mental state). This doesn't lead us anywhere better emotionally, and it certainly doesn't give our brains the chance to reset at all.

This would be like if you had the flu and you forced yourself to sprint really fast around the block and then yelled at yourself the whole time for not running faster. You probably wouldn't do this, and if you did, it wouldn't make you feel very good, and it wouldn't make the flu go away any faster. In fact, you might just make yourself feel a whole lot worse!

So why do we treat ourselves in this way? Why don't we recognize what's going on with our own brains and emotional states more, and take the time to pause and reset?

A lot of people have an unexamined notion that what's going on with their brains isn't really affecting their bodies, but this clearly isn't true. Scientific studies have shown us that when our brains feel stressed, our bodies feel stressed out, too. Our hearts can beat faster, our immune systems can weaken, our sleep can be affected, and chronic stress can actually shrink our brains (Ross 2020). In other words:

The thoughts we think affect our brains and our bodies.

While stress can *negatively* impact our bodies, having a more positive mindset can actually *improve* how our bodies function and perform.

Neuroscience nugget: Across 80 different scientific studies, researchers discovered that thinking positive thoughts and having an optimistic outlook had a "remarkable effect on physical health." They "examined overall longevity, survival from a disease, heart health, immunity, cancer outcomes, pregnancy outcomes, pain tolerance, and other health topics. It seemed that those who had a more optimistic outlook did better and had better results than those who were pessimistic" (Watson, Fraser, and Ballas n.d.).

So, knowing all this, let's practice by shifting our thoughts in a gentler, more positive way, a little bit at a time.

Start with Feeling Cozy

To use this tool, all you have to do is imagine a blanket. That's it—just picture a big fluffy blanket, whatever looks extra comfy and cozy to you. Take a second to imagine this.

I call this **The Kindness Blanket**. It's warm, cozy, and fluffy; it's a color you find calming or perhaps it's a color that you really like. When you wrap this blanket around yourself, you feel instantly soothed. You feel comforted. You feel relaxed. You feel safe. You feel like it's okay to relax right into it.

Wrap this imaginary fluffy **Kindness Blanket** around you and start to form some comforting, soothing little thoughts for yourself to think. I call these **micro-thoughts** as they help walk you over to a more positive place without causing too much mental resistance.

Sometimes, when you try to leap over to a thought like "I am such an amazing person!" from a place where you've been thinking "I'm such a mess and everything I do is wrong," it just doesn't stick because you just can't connect with it emotionally. It's not to say you won't get there in time, it's just way too uncomfortable a jump for your brain to make in the beginning, when you have been used to thinking more negatively about yourself. Your brain may want to argue, "I am clearly not amazing at all!" back at you, and now you're just fighting with your own brain.

Instead, practice walking yourself over with tinier, easier, positive thoughts that you don't feel a negative reaction to. You'll know when you find one because it will be easy for you to repeat it to yourself and the wording will feel easy to you. You can try some of the ones out below for size. Feel free to re-write them in a way that best suits your own brain or come up with a few new ones that work for you.

Here are some **micro-thoughts** to try out while you're wearing **The Kindness Blanket**:

"I'm figuring things out one step at a time."

"I don't need to push through things right now. I can take a break and rest for a while."

"If I let myself calm down a little, everything will feel much easier for me to do."

"I'm learning to let myself breathe into calmer feelings a little more each day."

"I'm learning to see calming down as a way I can be kinder to myself."

"I am changing my self-talk a little bit at a time."

"Every new step I take in a positive direction will lead me to a different outcome."

When you wrap **The Kindness Blanket** around you, it helps you connect to the beautiful and loving parts of yourself more. When you learn to go gentle in your thoughts toward yourself, it helps you see the world around as more beautiful, too.

So the next time you start to feel bad, cover yourself with a little kindness first.

Worksheet: Write it out!

Imagine a big comfy blanket. When you wrap it around yourself, you can remember to be gentle and kind to yourself in the way you speak to yourself. Write out five to ten kind and gentle thoughts you can soothe yourself with:

1. . . . .

2. . . . .

3. . . . .

4. . . . .

5. . . . .

6. . . . .

7. . . . .

8. . . . .

9. . . . .

10. . . . .

THE SELF-TALK METER

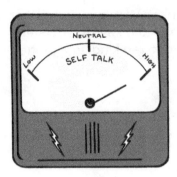

Your **self-talk** is comprised of the thoughts that you're thinking about yourself frequently, whether you realize it or not.

The Self-Talk Meter can help you get a better idea of what kinds of things you tend to say to yourself about *yourself*. If we're saying thousands of harsh and critical words to ourselves about ourselves all day long, it's bound to have a negative emotional effect on our daily moods.

In other words, the way we talk to ourselves is important.

Neuroscience nugget: Did you know that 70% of our daily thoughts are negative self-talk thoughts? After conducting a two-week study where business students were asked to record all of their thoughts in a "brutally honest" style, Dr Raj Raghunathan concluded from the results that daily "'mental chatter,' so to speak—is mostly (up to 70%) negative, a phenomenon that could be referred to as negativity dominance." He believes that: "Deep down, it turns out that people are much more self-critical, pessimistic, and fearful than they let out in their conscious thoughts" (Raghunathan 2013).

While no one can think positive thoughts *all* of the time (this would be a really unrealistic and unfair expectation to have of yourself), we can learn to *gradually* shift the percentage of how many positive thoughts we are generating throughout the day.

In other words, we don't have to go to "extremes" over changing our thought patterns and we don't have to change things instantly, either. You can go at your pace with this process. Even just adding in a few kinder thoughts toward yourself each day will make a little difference over time.

Think...percentages!

> **Neuroscience nugget:** Changing our thought patterns may be trickier than it sounds. As Andrew Newberg and Mark Waldman, authors of "Why this word is so dangerous to say or hear," explain: "When doctors and therapists teach patients to turn negative thoughts and worries into positive affirmations, the communication process improves and the patient regains self-control and confidence. But there's a problem: the brain barely responds to our positive words and thoughts." The solution to this **negativity bias**? "We must repetitiously and consciously generate as many positive thoughts as we can." Consistency is essential to changing self-talk in a way that sticks (Newberg and Waldman 2012).

Where Negative Self-Talk Comes From

Growing up, some of us had parents, caregivers, or other adults in our lives who may not have been very aware of how they were talking to themselves, and their own negative self-talk may have spilled out onto us as well. As kids, we may have internalized some of the harsh and negative things that were said to us by grown-ups because we may have believed their words to be true. Sometimes, negative self-talk is passed down through many generations until someone actively decides to change the self-talk pattern for good.

It's also possible that as we grew up, we may have had friends, partners, or peers who influenced our self-talk in a negative way. We may have also experienced traumatic or abusive situations that impacted how we learned to talk to ourselves, too.

It can be very helpful to discover the roots of your self-talk by going to therapy to spend a little time figuring these things out, as our self-talk often stems from different experiences over many years. Some clients find EMDR (Eye Movement Desensitization and Reprocessing) Therapy and trauma-based therapy to be especially helpful for processing past traumatic experiences, while other modalities of therapy, including cognitive behavioral therapy and rational emotive behavioral therapy, can be very helpful for changing patterns of thought (see: **Resources**).

However, no matter where your self-talk may come from, you can, right now, start to write some new gentler and more encouraging phrases to say to yourself more frequently.

You can now learn to begin to speak to yourself with more kindness, a little bit at a time.

Starting now, you can give yourself a little more of the praise, soothing, and encouragement that you have always deserved.

Your Meter and How It Moves

To begin with, imagine a meter with a needle that swings from one end to the other, which looks like this:

Most of us move up and down the meter frequently throughout the day, depending on how we're feeling about ourselves and how we feel about the things we happen to be doing.

On the **high** end, you might have really motivating and positive self-talk going on, like something an inspirational basketball coach might call out to you from the sidelines: "You've got this!" "Keep up the good work!" "You can do it!" When we hear this kind of encouragement, it tends to have a really motivational effect on us.

In the middle, there's a **neutral** setting for your self-talk, which sounds more like a logical observer of facts. If the **neutral** coach was watching you play a game, they would say things like, "You win some, you lose some" and "Some things you did really well and other things we can practice tomorrow." When you hear this kind of talk, it probably doesn't tip you over emotionally, and it may even calm you down a little. Your motivation level most likely lands somewhere in the middle.

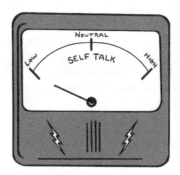

Then, over on the **low** end of this meter, this is when you have some really negative and critical self-talk going on. This is stuff a super-harsh basketball coach would yell at you from the sidelines: "What's wrong with you?" "That was awful!" "Everyone was counting on you and you screwed up!" "You're the worst!" and all sorts of non-helpful phrases like this. As a result, you may now feel completely unmotivated, and you're most likely feeling emotionally wonky as a result.

Your **Self-Talk Meter** is directly wired to your **Motivational Meter**.

Lots of positive self talk = Increased motivation

Lots of negative self talk = Decreased motivation

So, if you're feeling unmotivated, start to observe the way you're talking to yourself throughout the day. Become a mindful observer of the words you're using toward yourself on a regular basis. Listen to what you're saying to yourself, more of the time.

When we start to become more observant of our own thoughts, the thoughts we think will naturally start to change.

Notice the Little Notches

Let's take a few examples from clients and see how they moved their **Self-Talk Meters** up a few notches. After saying things to themselves on the low end of the meter, these clients wrote out different statements they could think until they got to the higher end of the meter, where their self-talk felt much more encouraging and motivating to them.

Client's task: Filling out an expenses report.

Low level: "I am doing a terrible job at this. I can't believe I lost that one receipt, what was I thinking? I am such an idiot."

Mid-notch: "I guess I can work on saving more paperwork for next time, but I still might forget."

Middle level: "I kept track of some things well and I didn't keep track of others."

Mid-notch: "I am learning how to track expenses in a better way each time."

High level: "I did a good job at tracking most things this month, I am learning more each time, and at least now I am done for this month. I can finally let myself take a break! I did it!"

Here's another example:

Client's task: Writing a paper.

Low level: "My professor is going to hate what I wrote. I am terrible at writing and I'm awful at time management."

Mid-notch: "I really struggled to plan out my time and I am worried I didn't edit it enough and I'll get a bad grade."

Middle level: "I'm glad it's over; however, next time I will leave more time to edit things."

Mid-notch: "Writing that paper took a lot out of me, but at least I got to the end of it."

High level: "I finished my paper by the deadline, which is really great and an improvement. I'm so proud of myself! I feel relieved that it's over. I can really have fun now and enjoy the rest of the weekend."

You can see from these two examples how a person can either walk themselves down to low, or walk themselves from low to high, depending on the little thoughts they are choosing to think along the way. If you catch yourself at a mid-notch, you could start to head back up on the meter just by thinking a different tiny thought.

The Sounds of Self-Talk

Sometimes, there is a tendency for us to use negative **extreme words** when our self-talk is at the low end of the meter.

Here are some common extreme words that tend to compile **negative self-talk** that you might catch yourself thinking when you're being overly harsh toward yourself:

* **Always:** You always screw up; you always forget things...
* **Never:** You never remember anything; you never get things right...
* **Why can't you:** Why can't you be like so-and-so? Why can't you do it right the first time?...
* **You used to:** You used to be better at such and such; you used to do that well and now you don't...
* **Negative labeling:** Using harsh, mean words to describe ourselves or something we've done—"idiot," "loser," "disaster," "failure," etc...
* **You aren't enough:** You aren't [fill in the blank] enough; you don't do enough; you'll never be enough...

Watch out for these negative extreme words as they can cause us to feel very intense emotions, and they also tend to sink our sense of self-esteem quickly.

Harsh words = Harsh emotions

Sometimes, if you can't think of motivational things to tell yourself right away, it can be helpful to aim for more **neutral self-talk** types of phrases to move up a few notches. These **neutralizing phrases** tend to lead us to calmer emotions and can often stabilize our **Self-Talk Meter.**

Neutral self-talk = Neutral emotions

Neutral self-talk thoughts, which put us in the middle of our meter, can include these types of calming, more balanced phrases that you might say to yourself:

* **It is what it is:** An acceptance of what's happening right now and allowing it to be how it is.
* **Things are temporary:** Things change constantly. Our situations, our feelings change. What you're feeling right now will change, too.
* **I can't control others but I can control what I think right now:** Go back to your sense of agency and let go of the things you can't control.
* **Every morning is a chance for me to reset myself and start again:** The sun still rises each morning, no matter what that day before was like. Each new morning is a chance to reset, start again, and have a new experience.
* **I am just going to breathe into this feeling for a little while:** Acknowledge and accept your feelings as they happen by breathing into them instead of trying to push them away.

Once you've practiced repeating these neutralizing self-talk thoughts for a while, and you are starting to feel calmer as a result, you can start ramping up your self-talk toward the high end of the meter. This is where you can really start to motivate yourself with what you're saying.

Positive self-talk tends to contain these types of motivational phrases that you can say to yourself to boost yourself way up to the high end of the meter:

* **Keep going:** This is your own resiliency talking to you and it is saying, "Keep it up!" "Keep going!" "Keep moving forward a little at a time and you'll get there!"
* **You've done so much to be proud of:** Remind yourself you've done so much already and you'll do more things ahead.
* **You're learning and growing:** This is your inner strength reminding you to keep trying, "I am learning so much with each step I take" and "With every step I take, I am helping myself grow."
* **You've figured things out:** You've figured many things out, you continue to figure things out as they happen, and you'll figure many things out again. You may even think, "I am getting better and better at figuring things out."
* **Good things can happen in the future:** This is where your self-soothing kicks in: "It will be okay," "It will all work out somehow," "Things tend to sort themselves out over time," "I can get to my goal if I just move forward a little at a time."
* **Look how far you've come:** This gives you some perspective on your own journey and how it's been successful in many ways that you might not realize. "Look how far I've come from where I started," "I have made so much progress in so many different areas of my life," and other types of self-reflective phrases can really provide some motivational turbo-boosts.
* **You are enough:** This is where we can reassure and nurture ourselves by remembering our own worth: "You are enough," "You are good enough the way you are," "You do enough," "You will be enough," and "You are always enough."

Motivational words = Motivating emotions

Reading that last list of motivating self-talk phrases, did you start to feel your mood lift just a little bit? Play around with a few of your own, custom-tailor the wording of a few positive phrases, until you start to feel that positive shift happening for you.

When Negative Self-Talk Spills Out

The words we say to ourselves all day long can sometimes spill out onto others, even if we don't intend them to. If you're saying a lot of **negative extreme words** to yourself all day long, it can be altogether too easy to suddenly say these types of negative phrases to people around you when you get stressed out (for example: "You never take out the trash!" or "Why can't you be more like so-and-so?").

Saying these types of **extreme words** will most likely cause the same intensely harsh emotions in others as they do in you when you say them to yourself.

However, you can just as easily boost up the people around you with kind, motivating, and encouraging words that can inspire happier emotions to happen. You just have to remember to frequently charge up your own self-talk first, so you have enough motivational energy to motivate and encourage others around you.

Turbo Boost vs. Jump Start

Other people and circumstances can sometimes bump us up on the meter once in a while, but they can't provide the charge to keep us there consistently. We have to do that for ourselves.

It can helpful to realize:

Waiting for outside praise is not a consistent way to get yourself over to the high end of the meter.

Instead of waiting for outside motivation, learn to drive yourself where you want to go more consistently. Say lots of motivational things to yourself each day and you'll get yourself there faster. And when others join in with some outside encouragement, it will feel more like a turbo-boost rather than a jump-start.

Turn the Harsh Talk Down

If you find you are struggling at first to introduce **motivational self-talk** into your daily self-talk stream, simply quieting down your **negative self-talk** a little is usually enough to improve how you're feeling.

As psychiatrist David D. Burns once wrote: "As you learn to stop haranguing yourself, you will begin to feel much better" (Burns 1981, p.80).

Once you turn that **negative self-talk** down a notch, your feelings of self-esteem will naturally start to rise as a result. Sprinkle in some **positive self-talk,** and you can turn your mood around even faster.

You can change your thoughts, a little at a time.

You're already doing it, right now.

Keep up the good work!

Worksheet: Write it out!

Pick a particular subject or task that you want to improve your **self-talk** on. Then, walk yourself up, one tiny thought at a time, from the low end to the high end of the **Self-Talk Meter**, filling in all the notches in between. The high end includes motivational and encouraging self-talk, the middle encompasses neutral self-talk, while the low end includes harsh and critical self-talk. The mid-notches are the in-between phrases moving you up or down between the main settings.

Client's task: Filling out an expenses report.

Low level: "I am doing a terrible job at this. I can't believe I lost that one receipt, what was I thinking? I am such an idiot."

Mid-notch: "I guess I can work on saving more paperwork for next time, but I still might forget."

Middle level: "I kept track of some things well and I didn't keep track of others."

Mid-notch: "I am learning how to track expenses in a better way each time."

High level: "I did a good job at tracking most things this month, I am learning more each time, and at least now, I am done for this month. I can finally let myself take a break! I did it!"

Now, it's your turn. Give it a try!

Subject:

Low level: . . . .

Mid-notch: . . . .

Middle level: . . . .

Mid-notch: . . . .

High level: . . . .

THE EVIDENCE INVESTIGATOR

We have the biggest effect on our own minds. This is not to diminish the effect of other people's feedback, as their words can move us up and down on The **Self-Talk Meter**, one way or the other. However, their words can't consistently change our meter's set point—we are the ones who must do that for ourselves. And we do that by how we talk to ourselves, all day long.

For example, let's imagine your supervisor tells you that you did a great job on a project and how happy she was that you finished it by the deadline, and it helps move you temporarily up to the high end of **The Self-Talk Meter**. "She said I did a great job on that project so that must mean I'm doing well at work!" you might think after hearing her praise, which may raise your **Self-Talk Meter** to high.

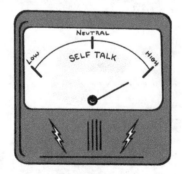

Do you stay at the high end for very long? If you aren't actively generating your own positive self-talk thoughts about finishing projects or your own abilities, and if you haven't built up a lot of previous self-talk on this particular subject before, **The Self-Talk Meter** might start to fall to neutral.

And then, here's where things can sometimes get emotionally wonky for people. If you actively begin to introduce negative self-talk, such as, "Maybe she didn't really mean what she said because she hasn't really read it yet" or "I probably won't do as well on the next project and she'll be disappointed," and now you've sent your meter plummeting down to low.

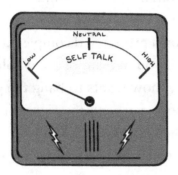

Your self-talk, which had previously been on the higher end (or in the middle) due to the compliment, has taken a negative turn: "She probably said she was happy I met the deadline because she really thought I wouldn't meet the deadline at all," you say to yourself, now engaging your pesky inner critic who chimes in: "Yeah—that's true! You've never been good at finishing things on time! You're really awful at deadlines!"

And now, you probably feel terrible as a result of all this negative self-criticism, and all this may have happened over the course of only a few minutes...even *after* receiving a compliment that boosted you way up high!

Defend Your Right to Feel Good

I often compare this "turning a compliment into an insult" problem to becoming your own **Negativity Lawyer** who is building up a solid case against yourself to feel completely awful. Because that's the Negativity Lawyer's main goal: to completely sink your mood and self-esteem meter all the way down to low.

The Negativity Lawyer is always searching for "bad" evidence, which is evidence that you somehow did a "bad job," or you are somehow a "bad person," so that you will feel bad as a result.

If you have this negative thought pattern going on, you can start to become more mindfully aware of it, and learn to shift it gradually.

To understand how it works, imagine the above scenario playing out in an imaginary courtroom inside your mind:

Situation: You did well on a project and completed it by the deadline. Your supervisor complimented you in front of the whole team.

Your brain, the **Judge**, now wants to bang the gavel and file this memory away as "happy" so it can send the signals to your brain to release happy-inducing brain chemicals as a result.

Unfortunately, this is when the Negativity Lawyer interrupts the process:

> Negativity Lawyer: "I object! Your supervisor clearly said she was happy you met the deadline because she thought you wouldn't meet the deadline at all!"

And then there's silence in the courtroom because now your brain doesn't know where to file this memory at all. Is it positive or negative? It seemed positive before, but now it seems negative. Your brain is now a little confused by this strange twist of logic.

> Negativity Lawyer: "And furthermore, you've never been good at meeting deadlines your whole life. Ever since that time you turned in your sixth grade science project one week late!"

Your brain is now frozen in confusion. If only you now had your own counsel to stand up and argue in your defense! If you had your own **Defense Attorney** searching for "good" evidence instead of "bad," the imaginary courtroom scene might look like this instead:

> Negativity Lawyer: "And furthermore, you've never been good at

meeting deadlines your whole life. Ever since that time you turned in your sixth grade science project late!"

Your Defense Attorney: "That's ridiculous! You had the flu in sixth grade and that's why you were out for a week. Besides, you were just a little kid! You're grown up now, you're not a little kid anymore. And clearly, your supervisor wouldn't have gone out of her way to compliment you in front of the team if she meant to insult you. She meant what she said: you did a good job. Accept it!"

Your Brain/Judge: "Objection overruled! This is clearly a happy memory and you are now permitted to feel happy. Case closed."

And then, ideally, you would let yourself feel happy as a result!

Investigate the Evidence

If you find yourself frequently trying to negate good things that happen to you or that people say to you, it can be helpful to use the **Evidence Investigator**. This is like training your brain to be your own **Defense Attorney**.

Let's say your friend just told you, "I like how you decorated your new apartment. It looks really artsy and fun."

You start to feel happy. Then, your **Negativity Lawyer** pipes in with, "She is just saying the word 'artsy' because she doesn't like your apartment at all, she's just being nice."

This completely illogical thought now starts to bother you. After your friend leaves, you might want to try using the **Evidence Investigator** to tease out how you are getting stuck, so that you can start to feel better.

Question Any Strange Logic

Start by writing out the statement you would like to challenge:

Statement: "She just said that to be nice, she wouldn't have said 'artsy' if she really liked it."

Now, ask yourself questions coming to your own defense:

Do I have evidence that this statement is true?

Let's say you answer "yes" to this question. Then, write out what exactly you think your evidence is. Ask yourself the following question:

What is the specific relevant evidence that this is true?

My friend is really nice so she wouldn't say if she hated the décor; she might use another word instead, something like "artsy."

Often, when you simply write out what you think your "relevant evidence" is, you may quickly realize how flimsy your own argument sounds on paper. You might now think, "Yeah, this doesn't make any sense... I don't even know why I thought this at all." And then, it's easy to move on to other thoughts.

However, let's say you're still feeling stuck. You would continue your investigation:

Do I really think this specific evidence applies here?

Well, probably not, she tends to say what she means.

Do I have any evidence that it might *not* be true?

She tends to like fun things so it's probably a compliment, not an insult.

Are there any other possibilities that might be true here?

Yes, she could have thought it was nice, she could have thought it was okay. She could have thought nothing about it at all. All these outcomes are okay.

Am I basing this statement I'm thinking on facts, feelings, or opinions?

It is a feeling I am having and my feelings aren't the same as facts.

Do I want to continue to believe this statement?

No. I can see now I just jumped to a strange conclusion that doesn't make much sense.

What's something else I can think about this situation now?

It's nice of my friend to notice things I've done to my place as I put a lot of work into fixing it up. I can feel proud of what I've done.

By now, you've convinced yourself to feel better about the situation. You're on your way to happier feelings!

Build Up Your Defense

Here are some questions to ask yourself when you feel the urge to turn something good (or neutral) into something bad inside your thoughts. You don't have to use all these questions; simply select a few, and see where it goes from there.

Pick from a few questions off of this list the next time you feel yourself getting stuck on a particular negative thought:

* Do I have any specific relevant evidence this is true?
* Do I have any evidence this might *not* be true?
* Are there any other possibilities that might be true other than what I am thinking?
* Is there a necessary reason I might have for seeing the negative in this situation?
* Am I basing this on facts, opinions, or feelings?
* Are all my feelings always true?
* Do I want to continue to believe this statement I'm telling myself?
* What is some "good" evidence I can find here instead of "bad"?
* How else can I see this situation?

Question that strange negative logic a little bit more as it appears. Don't let the **Negativity Lawyer** win every case hands down. Give yourself a fair trial instead.

Defend your right to feel good more of the time. Then, actually allow yourself to feel it!

Worksheet: Write it out!

Take a situation that happened to you recently. Write out the negative statement that you formed after it happened. Then, investigate the evidence by answering the questions below.

Negative statement: . . . .

. . . .

Do I have any specific relevant evidence this is true?

. . . .

. . . .

Do I have any evidence this might *not* be true?

. . . .

. . . .

Am I basing this on facts, opinions, or feelings?

. . . .

. . . .

What is some "good" evidence I can find here instead of "bad"?

. . . .

. . . .

How else can I see this situation?

. . . .

. . . .

THE INSTANT REPLAY

While we can sometimes beat ourselves up with the words we tell our-selves, we also can beat ourselves up with the past images that we replay in our minds.

How often do we mentally replay our greatest mistakes, regrets, and/or embarrassing moments throughout our days, weeks, years? How often is our brain tempted to put on our least favorite past video on our mental movie screen even though we logically know that viewing it again leads us nowhere good emotionally? After listening to many clients struggle to stop this habit of replaying self-esteem-sinking memories on a loop, I developed **The Instant Replay** tool.

It is based on this simple question:

What types of scenes from your past are you frequently replaying inside your mind?

In other words, are you choosing to rewatch your "greatest hits" or your "most cringeworthy moments" on your mental movie screen? Whichever one you decide to watch on a frequent basis has a completely different effect on how you feel.

Neuroscience nugget: In a year-long study conducted in 2019, researchers found that remembering positive things from the past helped participants lower their cortisol levels and improved their general resiliency over time. "We found that positive memory specificity was associated with lower morning cortisol and fewer negative self-cognitions during low mood over the course of one year," explained researchers (Askelund *et al.* 2019, p.265).

Since our brains are naturally wired toward a **neural negativity bias,** back from a primitive time where we had to be alert to dangers like bears, snakes, and tigers, we often replay our most negative "worst" moments as a way to warn ourselves against repeating them. Did you step on a pile of leaves once and almost get bitten by a lurking snake? Your brain might replay this "snake" video frequently to make sure you never get bitten by a snake again in the future. Every time you see a pile of leaves, it will launch right into an instant replay of "When Snakes Attack"!

While this might work well for avoiding snakes, this feature of our brains doesn't really help us when "Embarrassing High School Cafeteria Moment" is replayed over and over (and over) again. Replaying these types of mental videos only sinks our mood *and* our self-esteem. If there was important information to be gained from the negative cafeteria experience, we probably learned it the first few times we watched the mental video, not the 1,000,000th time we replayed it (decades after high school ended).

The good news is, you can change this habit, one mental movie at a time.

Disaster Movies

When I work with clients who are getting stuck in "anxiety loops," they typically describe it as the mental "replaying" of a negative event, circumstance, or criticism someone once told them. It's like their mental video is stuck in an endless loop, and the more they watch it, the more they start to feel negative emotions and low self-esteem as a result.

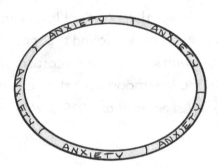

One client couldn't stop her urge to **instant replay** the scene of a recent relationship break-up, over and over again. It had been many months since the break-up had occurred, but she felt she was getting stuck in an instant replay loop.

"I need help breaking this anxious cycle," she said in a session, "I can't stop thinking about the awkward conversation I had with my ex over and over again."

When you catch yourself in this type of instant replay cycle, ask yourself: "Is there an actionable item I can take away from rewatching this scene again?"

Her answer to this question was: "Not really. I wish I had said a few things differently, but I can see that I just felt hurt in that moment and so I was emotional as a result."

Then, ask yourself: "Is rewatching this scene again helping me right now or not helping me?"

Her answer was: "It is definitely *not* helping me!"

So then, ask yourself, "What future emotions will I feel as a result of rewatching this scene?"

Her answer was: "I will feel terrible and awful, like I've wasted more time and energy on something I don't need to revisit ever again."

Then, ask yourself: "How do I want to feel instead? Describe how you want to feel in the future."

She answered: "I want to feel like I can put this behind me and move on to calmer feelings. I want to feel like I'm getting back on track with things I need to do and moving toward doing things I want to do more of."

Fast-Forward to a Future Scene

When you're stuck in a **negative replay loop,** try to focus your thoughts on what you want to *feel* in the future instead. It can be helpful to write this out as a **"Positive Future Scene"** on paper and then reread it as needed, to give yourself a little boost. In this way, you're fast-forwarding to where you want to see yourself in the future.

Client's "Positive Future Scene": Six months after the break-up, I see myself traveling to places that I've always wanted to visit. I have more time now, and I can plan out my time however I want now. I see myself feeling confident. I see myself feeling really proud of myself for doing so well and making so much progress. I see myself doing so many things I never thought I could do on my own. I am so much stronger now.

Picture yourself feeling the feelings you want to feel. What does that look like to you? What are you doing? What more enjoyable feelings are you having? Hold on to that image and revisit it frequently. In this way, we are learning to soothe ourselves with our own imagination in a more positive way.

A few weeks after completing this journaling exercise, the client announced she had given up mentally replaying the scene of the break-up.

She said, "I told myself I could replay the scene of the break-up but I would probably spend all night crying and feeling terrible as a result. So, if I wanted to spend all night crying and feeling terrible, I could replay the break-up scene in my head. And then, somehow, I didn't feel like doing it again! Because I want to picture myself feeling better now, not worse."

When you picture where you want to end up emotionally, your brain can help get you there.

Your Greatest Hits Montage

Wouldn't it be more beneficial to our moods and self-esteem to choose more inspiring moments from our past to play in our mental movie theater more of the time? Instead of replaying your most cringeworthy moments, wouldn't it be more helpful to replay your **greatest hits** once in a while?

Dallas Cowboys coach, Tom Landry, made each of his players rewatch their greatest hits as a way to inspire and motivate them before games. He explained to his players, "We only replay your winning plays!" (Buckingham and Goodall 2019). He believed that replaying his players' best moments would motivate them to **recreate** those winning moments again. And it worked!

Learn to motivate yourself by remembering past things that you've done well.

Let's pause the **neural negativity bias** trend for a few moments by choosing what we want to watch on **instant replay** in our minds right now. Start by forming a list of your own **personal greatest hits** that you can revisit and reread whenever you need to give your self-esteem and confidence a little boost!

Worksheet: Write it out!

Make a list of your greatest hits. They can be small wins, big wins, something happy, something triumphant, something fun, or anything you've experienced recently that was enjoyable to you. And then, the next time you need a boost, pick one of your greatest hits to watch in your mental movie theater. Remember Coach Landry's mantra: "We only replay your winning plays!"

My greatest hits:

. . . .

. . . .

. . . .

. . . .

. . . .

Now write out a few "future greatest hits" you want to imagine experiencing:

. . . .

. . . .

. . . .

. . . .

. . . .

CHAPTER ROUND-UP

☑ Cover yourself in kindness.

☑ Learn what different types of **self-talk** sound like.

☑ The thoughts we think affect our brains and bodies.

☑ Motivate yourself by replaying your **greatest hits.**

☑ Defend your right to feel good more often.

☑ Fast-forward to a **positive scene** in the future.

CHAPTER 2

When You Want to Boost Your Confidence...

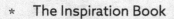

* The Inspiration Book
* The Seesaw
* The Multifaceted Gemstone

* The Story Selector
* The Inner Hero
* The Cartoon Animal

THE INSPIRATION BOOK

As kids, we intuitively knew how to use our creativity and imaginations to make us feel better. We colored in coloring books and relaxed ourselves by choosing different shades of crayons. We played with sand and felt proud of the castles we made. We put on capes and crowns and had a whole lot of fun being silly. Now, as adults, we sometimes forget that there are many ways to utilize this amazing imagination tool that we still possess.

Instead, we tend to overuse our imagination to picture future disasters and stressful problems, and under-use our imagination to picture things that are delightful, creative, or inspiring to do.

Learn to use your imagination to picture more delights, instead of more disasters.

You still have the exact same creative imagination inside of you that you had as a child. It didn't go anywhere, even though you might think that it did; it's still there waiting for you to use it in fun ways. Remember dancing around the living room? Singing songs that you made up? Drawing until the markers ran dry? It was easy to get lost inside our heads when we were kids, and our heads were often an enjoyable place to get lost in.

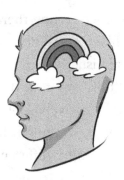

As adults, using our creative imaginations can help us picture what we want to happen in the future, instead of what we don't want to happen. It can also help us remember that we have many interests, skills, and abilities that we can use in a relaxing way.

Neuroscience nugget: Researchers at the Georgia Institute of Technology studied the brain patterns of 100 participants who were told to "daydream" during MRI scans. The participants were then given tests to measure their intellectual and creative abilities, and were also told to rate how often their thoughts "drift off" into daydreams each day. They found that "Those who reported more frequent daydreaming scored higher on intellectual and creative ability and had more efficient brain systems measured in the MRI machine" (Maderer 2017). When we let ourselves daydream, we can practice mental flexibility in a creative way that can help our brains perform better.

Sometimes, the reason why we're not tapping into our imagination and creativity more often is simply because we've forgotten that we can.

Make an Inspiration Book

One way you can start to practice getting there again is to make an **Inspiration Book**. This can look like a small notebook that you carry around in your bag, or, if you're more visually inclined, you can drag photos into a folder called "Inspiration Book" on your desktop instead.

As you go through each day, actively look for things that inspire you. For instance, if Paris inspires you, you might list a few French song lyrics down in your notebook. If you enjoy different types of food, you might collect names of dishes you'd like to learn how to make. If you like design, you might start taking photos of different objects that inspire you, even if it's something as small as a table lamp or a salt shaker. If you like to write, you might jot down a few memorable quotes from books you've read or conversations that you've had.

If you have multiple interests, collect a long list of different things that interest you; there's no need to overanalyze what you are collecting.

When you look at all the words and images you've collected at the end of the week, your brain might naturally start to see patterns connecting all the different types of things that you like, which can lead to insight.

Here are some questions you can ask yourself to figure out what inspires you:

* What things and places am I drawn to visually?
* What images bring me joy to look at?
* What sounds, smells, colors, and objects are pleasing to me?
* Which locations would be fun to explore?
* What activities can I picture myself trying?
* What things did I delight in or enjoy when I was little kid?

When I was a little kid, I used to have a poster of a pair of ballet pointe shoes on my wall. I used to stare at that poster every night and daydream about how fun it would be to dance on stage someday. While I don't dance anymore, I can still easily drift off into enjoyable dancing daydreams when I hear inspiring pieces of music.

What frequent daydreams did you get lost in as a little kid? What were you doing in them? What good feelings did they inspire you to feel?

Practice the feelings you want to feel by using your imagination more deliberately each day.

To begin with, start by collecting images and ideas that make you smile, and see where the inspiration leads you next...

Worksheet: Write it out!

Using your senses, write out 10 things today that inspire you. Look around for things that make you smile, things you feel drawn to, things that make you feel creative, or things that make you feel inspired! Try it every day for a week and see where the inspiration takes you.

This week, these 10 things inspired me:

1. . . . .

2. . . . .

3. . . . .

4. . . . .

5. . . . .

6. . . . .

7. . . . .

8. . . . .

9. . . . .

10. . . . .

☆

THE SEESAW

Over the years, as a therapist, I've often noticed that people in the exact same situations can have completely different perspectives on the exact same subject.

For instance, I'll ask a client who is job hunting if they are feeling stressed about it, and they'll say, "Oh no, I always get jobs, I'm not worried about finding one. Whenever I've needed a job, I've always found one."

However, if I ask another client in the exact same situation (even in the exact same line of work) the very same question, they'll say, "Jobs are impossible to find right now. There are no jobs. How am I ever going to get one when no one else is getting one?"

Or a client who is looking for a new relationship will announce, "There are absolutely no single people left in this city anywhere!" and another client who is also looking for a new relationship will instead proclaim, "There are millions of people in this city; it's only a matter of time until I meet someone."

Even two different clients who are trying to get tickets to the exact same event will say completely different things. One will say, "I'm not too worried about getting tickets. I'll just check this weekend and see what's available." And another will say, "I've been checking the website non-stop and everything is selling out and I know they're going to sell out before I even get a chance to buy them!"

How can the same subject produce such completely *different* takes from people?

The Different Sides of a Subject

Imagine a **Seesaw** in a playground. On one end of the seesaw are the words "lack of." When we are sitting high up on the "lack of" side, the "plenty of" side is down low. When we look around at the world on the "lack of" side of the seesaw, we see things through the lens of "scarcity." We might see an empty playground with very little around to entice us. Maybe we see one scrawny tree and some dirt on the ground, and that's about it.

Imagine that the other end of the seesaw is called "plenty of." When you're sitting high up on the "plenty of" side and you look around the playground, you see plenty of trees, lots of lush grass, plenty of things to do and explore. When you're on this side looking out onto the world, you see plenty of everything around you, and it's also easier to feel plenty of confidence, too.

Give your two sides of the seesaw names that do not cause much mental resistance in you to think about, for example: "plenty of/lack of," "abundant/scarce," or "a little of/a whole lot of." Whichever wording feels the easiest for you to use, try it out as you play around with this tool.

Start to look at a few subjects in your life, and try to figure out where you're sitting on the seesaw with them.

Different Seesaws for Different Subjects

Most of us are not *always* on one end of **The Seesaw** or always on the other end; it goes up and down frequently, depending on what *specific* subject we're thinking about. The seesaw also tips in different ways on different subjects for different people. For example, you may feel you have "plenty of friends and acquaintances" and a "lack of money each month." Your friend might think she has "plenty of great job options" but "no chance at ever finding a house to buy." People are all over the place on the seesaw, depending on what the subject is, and to whom you are speaking.

What subjects tend to tip you over to the "plenty of" side? What subjects tend to tip you right over to the "lack of" side? And what subjects land you somewhere in the middle?

Finding the Middle

In the middle of **The Seesaw** is the "neutral" setting where both ends are balanced equally. A neutral approach to the subject would be something like, "It's not scarce or abundant; it's somewhere in the middle."

For example, on the subject of money, someone on the middle of the seesaw might think, "Money comes and goes into my life. Sometimes I have a lot, sometimes I have a little." You can view the situation more calmly from the middle and see both ends of the seesaw without getting too tipped over emotionally.

The Scarcity Mindset

How do we get ourselves stuck in a **scarcity mindset**? Sometimes, it comes from our past experiences. If we grew up in a situation where resources were very hard to come by, we might feel like things are still hard to obtain, even when we're not kids anymore and things may have changed for us. In this way, we can get stuck in the "scarcity mindset" on certain subjects long after we've consistently had more than enough resources to survive and thrive.

In many cases, we may have learned "scarcity" stories from the people who raised us. Growing up, we may also have been told by many adults around us things like, "money is scarce" or "jobs are hard to find" or "it's hard to find a good partner" or "it's impossible to get into a good school," so much so that we adopted these types of core beliefs as our own.

It might take some time to shift your beliefs, especially ones you've held on to for a while, so it's helpful to remember to be kind and gentle to yourself during the process. Trust that you'll get there in time, and go at your own pace.

Tipping the Seesaw

When you start to feel yourself leaning toward the "lack of" side on a subject, try to ask yourself a few questions:

* What is it I actually want?
* What is an action I might take to get closer to where I want to go?
* What would be the first small step toward moving in that direction?

Remember, on the "plenty of" side of **The Seesaw** there's room for everyone to succeed, including you! It can be helpful to remember:

If all else fails to tip the seesaw, engage your natural sense of curiosity.

If you need help engaging your sense of curiosity, it can be helpful to try out a few of these tiny **micro-thoughts** to tip you over to the "plenty of" mindset:

"I wonder what that's like to experience."

"I wonder what steps I can take to get there."

"I wonder what that will feel like for me to do."

"I wonder if I really want that. I'm going to play around with that idea for a few days and see how it feels."

Curiosity allows us to pull back our perspective, to step outside of our insecurities, and to think, "What is it I really want to do, and how can I start to move in that direction?"

Map It Out

Write out a subject you would like to work on. For example:

Subject: Finding a new apartment.

Lack of: There are no apartments available right now, and the news says there is a housing shortage in the city. I will never find a new apartment and I will be stuck here forever.

Middle: There are always some apartments for rent, and there will always be new apartments for rent in the future that I can't predict right now.

Plenty of: Every week, there are many new possibilities to be explored and I am sure I will find a new place to live soon enough, if I just keep looking around.

In this way, you can practice tipping **The Seesaw** over a little more on the subjects that are making you feel stuck.

When you begin to see the world around you as having plenty of possibilities, you may now also be able to see pathways toward your goals you didn't even realize were there before.

As author Joseph Campbell once said: "Follow your bliss...and doors will open where you didn't know they were going to be" (quoted in Campbell, Moyers, and Tatge 2012).

Worksheet: Write it out!

To use **The Seesaw** tool, pick a subject that you tend to sit on the "lack of" side with. Ask yourself, "How can I shift my perspective on this subject a little?" Then, write your way over to the other side of the seesaw where the subject now feels more "plentiful" to you. For example:

Subject: Finding a new apartment.

Lack of: There are no apartments available right now, and the news says there is a housing shortage in the city. I will never find a new apartment and I will be stuck here forever.

Middle: There are always some apartments for rent, and there will always be new apartments for rent in the future that I can't predict right now.

Plenty of: Every week, there are many new possibilities to be explored and I am sure I will find a new place to live soon enough, if I just keep looking around.

Now, it's your turn:

Subject: . . . .

. . . .

Lack of: . . . .

. . . .

Middle: . . . .

. . . .

Plenty of: . . . .

. . . .

THE MULTIFACETED GEMSTONE

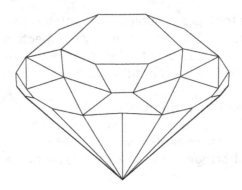

Sometimes, when we're experiencing feelings of low self-esteem, it's because we're trying to shrink our whole vast amazing human being-ness down into one tiny little box.

It's as though we are actively trying to make ourselves *smaller* instead of realizing how *expansive* our true natures are.

Sometimes, the box is a job title. Sometimes, it's a relationship title. Sometimes, it's a creative title, but it can be other things, too. Basically, it's when you don't fully accept that you are a complex person who does many things and has many different strengths, talents and interests, and instead, you attempt to define yourself with *only one thing* instead.

Unfortunately, this can lead to feelings of low self-esteem when the one thing you've defined yourself as isn't working out fast enough. For instance, if you only see yourself as an athlete, and you don't score any points in a big game, your feelings of self-esteem may start to sink because you don't see yourself as having a lot of self-worth outside of being an athlete. Or, if you only see yourself as an executive, and you don't get promoted right away, or, if you only see yourself as an actor, and you don't get the part you wanted, etc.... You can probably imagine hundreds of different variations on this very same theme.

In other words, you've put way too much weight and pressure entirely on that one thing, so much so, that it makes your feelings of self-worth feel very precarious as a result.

One way to remember this is to think of this equation:

You = Only one thing = Feelings of low self-esteem

However, you can now start to broaden your idea of what makes you...you!

You can now start expanding your definition of who you are, instead of shrinking that definition down.

When Your Job = Your Identity

A client came to see me because she was feeling anxious at her executive level job, and she wanted to find out why. Even though she was doing really well at her job, she felt a sense of unease, like she was going to "lose her job someday," even though there was no actual evidence that she would. After some sessions, she realized she had formed this equation:

Job = Identity

She said she felt like without her job, she was "was nothing and nobody." Even when she was clearly doing well at it and receiving praise from her co-workers, she couldn't enjoy any of it. She said that she had accidentally made this equation:

Losing job = Loss of identity

"I don't want to think like this at all," she said, "I just don't know who I am anymore outside of my job, and if I lose my job, I will feel like I'm nothing."

I pointed out that she didn't have a job when she was a kid—did she think she was "nothing" then?

"No, I didn't think that at all, I liked myself a lot back then," she said. I asked her what she liked to do as a kid, and she replied, "I loved to draw.

I drew all the time. And I also thought it would be fun to cook. When I was a teenager, I really liked watching food and travel shows."

I asked her, "Why not do try some of those things now? Aren't they a part of your personality still, even if it's been a while?"

Using the **Inspiration Book**, she spent the next few weeks detailing out things that inspired her outside of work. She quickly discovered that she still loved drawing and cooking as much as she did when she was younger. She decided to try out a bunch of new recipes, and she even started inviting friends over to try out what she had made. Over time, she started to take art classes on the weekends and was sketching a little each day. As she explored these things, she began to realize she was having "way less anxiety" at her job. She wasn't "overly focusing on it" as much throughout the week.

"I've started to remember all the sides to me that aren't job-related," she said, "I like all those sides to me a lot. I'm starting to feel more like myself again!"

She had expanded her definition of herself by accepting *more* of who she was.

How might this apply to you?

Change Your Own Equation

Whenever you link your entire self-worth or identity to just one thing, you're setting yourself up for feelings of low self-esteem. Whether it's being a CEO, an entrepreneur, a performer, a spouse, an executive, an academic, an athlete, an artist, a supervisor, a parent…one thing cannot possibly summarize your entire human being-ness. You are far, far, far bigger than that.

Here's an equation to remember:

$$You > Just\ one\ thing$$

You are greater than just one thing. We all are!

You Are a Multifaceted Gemstone

A few years ago, while on a road trip, I happened upon a small store full of beautiful natural rocks and natural gemstones. A tiny sign under one of the glittering jewels read: "Multifaceted gemstones are cut to maximize their natural beauty. This type of cut reflects the light from inside and out."

Later, when I was thinking of tools to explain expanding **self-definition**, I thought about that sign again and how it can also apply to people (not just rocks):

You are a multifaceted gemstone.

You have many different sides.

All of these different sides reflect the light

that comes from the inside and outside.

Start to appreciate *all* of your interests, roles, talents, strengths, passions, and skills. Write them all out on paper in a long list and read them to yourself.

All of what's written down—all of those sparkling facets—it's all part of the same amazing gem. You!

Worksheet: Write it out!

On the multifaceted gemstone below, write out different words that summarize you in each section of the stone. Fill up each section with a word (passions, interests, roles, skills, qualities, talents, etc.). See how they all come together and form one amazing gemstone:

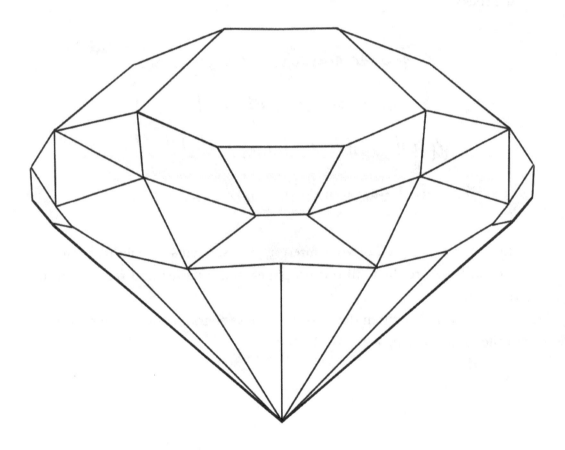

THE STORY SELECTOR

Have you ever had anyone point out that the story you're telling other people *about* yourself isn't really accurate or true?

For example, have you ever told someone a story about yourself as a chronically clumsy person who constantly breaks a lot of things, and someone you know interrupted you and said, "I don't think you're clumsy at all. That's not how I see you, you seem really calm and collected."

Or, you've told a story about yourself as someone who always forgets important details, and someone says, "I don't think you're forgetful, you usually have a really good memory."

Or, you've announced, "Sorry my car is always such mess!" to people just as they're getting in, and they've said, "What are you talking about?" or "For a messy car, this is pretty clean."

And then you had to pause and think, "Wait, what?" or "How can that be true?"

What this usually means is that the old negative story you have been telling people about yourself...could use a little adjusting. For example:

Old stories: I am messy. I am forgetful. I am clumsy.

You may have been telling old stories such as these for years, but you've never stopped to investigate whether they're actually true and/or based on current facts. You may also never have stopped to consider whether or not you want to continue telling these stories going forward, too.

If this is the case, you can ask yourself: "Are these old stories helping me or not helping me right now?"

Sometimes, the "old story" was never really all that accurate to begin with. It might have been **negative self-talk** that you told yourself so frequently that it formed into a **negative self-story**. And now that negative self-story might be keeping you from feeling the confidence that you really want to feel.

Change the Story

Often, the negative self-stories we've been telling about ourselves are running on auto-pilot, and it takes a little deliberate work to start to shift them in a completely new direction.

It can be helpful to take a few minutes each week to write out some "old stories" that you frequently catch yourself telling people. Then, think of some new stories you'd like to say instead. You can make a list like this:

Old stories	New stories
I am messy.	I am creative and I like to try new things out. I am learning how to organize things in shorter bursts.
I am forgetful.	I remember plenty of things each day and I'm getting better at writing things down more.
I am clumsy.	I am excited by life and I tend to move quickly. I am learning ways to find my balance more.

Add a few others and see how you can rewrite them to find the "good evidence" instead of the "bad evidence."

Old stories	New stories
I am bad with money.	There are many things I've already paid off. I am getting better at figuring out money each year.
I never know what to wear.	I like many styles of clothes and different designs and I'm starting to discover what I prefer.
I am really unorganized.	I am learning new ways to organize things and I am figuring out systems that work for me.

Now, as you're going about your day, and you want to tell everyone what a mess you are, you would ideally catch yourself, and think, "That's just an old story I'm telling about myself."

Catch Those Old Stories

When you hear yourself starting to tell a negative "old story" about yourself, here are the steps you can take:

1. Pause your words.
2. Say inside your mind, "That's just an old story" or simply, "Old story."
3. Remember the new story you want to tell.
4. Tell the new story instead.

While this may sound really simple, in reality, the process can sometimes feel very awkward and uncomfortable the first few times you do it. You might have to pause yourself mid-word, wait a few seconds, and then reroute yourself manually, like a GPS recalibrating directions when you start to make a wrong turn.

However, each time you practice, the whole thing will go a little smoother for you, until, one day, you'll find you've somehow left the old story behind. These self-stories we tell are just habits we've developed, and you can break any negative habit with a little determination and consistent focus.

> **Neuroscience nugget:** In a brain imaging study done at Dartmouth College, researchers found that a part of the brain called the frontostriatal pathway was "stronger and more active" in participants who described themselves as having positive qualities and values. Dr Robert Chavez noted that he only saw brain activity on the scans when people described themselves with positive terms, not negative ones. He explained that a strong and active frontostriatal pathway may be "driven by the positive aspects of your sense of self" (quoted in Almendrala 2017).

When we are actively selecting more **positive self-stories** to tell, we are rewiring our brains in a beneficial way.

The Uncomfortable Feelings of Change

One client kept wanting to bring up her "old story" about how "dumb" she was, even though she was the only one telling this story. In reality, she received a lot of praise about her intelligence and skills from others, but she wouldn't let herself believe any of it. The old story, however negative, felt so true and comfortable to her to tell that she hadn't taken the time to question it and to actively change it.

After using the **Evidence Investigator**, she began to realize her old story clearly wasn't helping her feel any better. So, she decided to write a new story:

Old story	New story
I am dumb.	I have figured many things out before and learned many new things before.
I don't have a graduate degree.	I have years of experience figuring things out and many valuable skills I have learned over the years.

As she learned to adjust her old story to her new one, she frequently felt what I describe as "The Uncomfortable Feelings of Change."

"It feels strange," she said, "I catch myself saying, 'I'm so dumb!' about a dozen times a day. And sometimes, I catch myself saying it to someone, and I have to stop myself mid-sentence and then it feels really uncomfortable."

"Yes, but it doesn't feel good to continue to tell the old story about yourself either," I said.

"Yeah, that feels way worse," she admitted.

When you're just starting to tell a new story about yourself, feeling "weird" about the new story you want to tell is a common feeling.

Change often causes anxiety. Change causes discomfort, even if the change is ultimately helping us out. But change is only temporary. It will pass.

This change anxiety often feels the most uncomfortable when it's right before a big shift. Ride those feelings out—get to the other side of the change anxiety, and you'll start to feel better emotionally on the other side. You could also remind yourself:

Once a new type of thinking no longer feels "new," it starts feeling less uncomfortable.

The more you practice, the easier it will feel to do.

In this client's case, it took her a few months of practicing the new story and of catching herself mid-old story to shift things. However, after a few months had passed, she realized she was no longer telling the old story to people at all.

"Wait a minute," she said in the middle of a session, "I just told you something I accomplished without saying bad things about my intelligence afterward!"

It was as though, in that moment, she fully realized she had finally left her old story behind.

"How does that feel?" I asked her.

"Really good! You know, I don't think I need that old story anymore," she laughed.

"You never did," I told her. It was true. She never really needed that story; she just had to realize it herself.

Take a second and think of a few old **self-stories** that you would like to change.

Start to tell the story you want to live instead.

Worksheet: Write it out!

Write out a few of your "old stories" that you would like to change. Then, rewrite them as gentler, kinder "new stories" you can start to tell yourself (and others) from now on instead. For example:

Old stories	New stories
I am messy.	I am creative and I like to try new things out. I am learning how to clean up in shorter bursts.
I am forgetful.	I remember plenty of things each day and I'm getting better at writing things down more.

Now, give it a try:

Old stories	New stories
. . . .	. . . .
. . . .	. . . .
. . . .	. . . .
. . . .	. . . .
. . . .	. . . .
. . . .	. . . .
. . . .	. . . .
. . . .	. . . .
. . . .	. . . .
. . . .	. . . .
. . . .	. . . .
. . . .	. . . .

THE INNER HERO

If you're going to be telling a new story, wouldn't you actually like to see yourself as the hero of your new story?

And so, following this line of thought, if you're the hero of your own story, you therefore have heroic values and strengths. What do those values and strengths look like? Let's investigate this and get to know our own **Inner Hero** a little more.

Which Heroes Do You Admire?

A helpful place to start is to think about some heroes you admire from fictional stories. When we think about the archetypal heroes in stories that we like to watch or read, it's easy to think about the heroic values that we're drawn to.

These heroic values might be things like:

Loyalty	Love
Respecting people/animals/ nature	Perseverance
	Family
Protecting others	Friendship
Generosity	Community
Kindness	Life-long learning
Bravery	Sense of justice

Honesty   Standing up for one's beliefs
Integrity

...as well as many other noble values.

Heroic strengths we might admire can include:

Courage   Inner calm
Resiliency   A strong moral compass
Honesty   Facing fears
Empathy   Highly motivated
Creativity   Optimism
Wisdom   Determination
Passion   Strong sense of humor
Accountability   Thinking outside of the box
Adaptability   Supporting those who are
Self-belief   different
Reliability   The ability to uplift others

...as well as many other heroic strengths.

The heroes we like in stories and movies don't all have the exact same personalities, qualities, values, physiques, or strengths. They look different, they act differently, they love differently; they even have different types of one-liners and catch phrases that they tend to say.

Which types of heroic strengths, qualities, and values resonate the most with you?

When you think about heroes doing heroic things in movies or books, specific scenes probably pop into your mind where they're defending people, showing kindness and compassion to others, or saving the day.

When you think about your life, what are some heroic past moments that pop into your mind? Start with smaller, everyday heroic moments. Did you defend a co-worker at your job? Did you teach someone how to do believe in themselves a little more? Did you help someone navigate a problem? Did you provide comfort to someone in need? How about all of the times you've been generous and kind to others? Aren't you showing a little courage right now by learning new ways to approach things?

Remember the times in your life when your own inner hero saved the day.

Neuroscience nugget: Researchers at a Canadian university took a sampling of 311 students and discovered that high self-esteem was linked to having "internal and interpersonal values." They also discovered that "people who place a higher weight on internal values tend to have higher self-liking and self-competency" (Kropp 2006, p.14).

When you focus on the positive strengths and values you already have, you can strengthen your sense of self more.

Start to picture yourself as the hero of an adventure that you're creating, one chapter at a time.

So, what does your **Inner Hero** look like?
Let's find out!

Worksheet: Write it out!

Take a few minutes to think about 3-5 specific heroes you admire in books and movies. Write out their values and strengths, and then write a few examples of scenes where these heroes displayed these qualities:

Hero	Values and strengths	Story examples
Example: Spiderman	Funny, kind, never gives up	Saves his friends' lives

Now, list out your own heroic values and strengths. Then, write out a few everyday examples from your own life where you displayed these qualities:

Your values and strengths	Life examples
Example: Kindness, determination	I helped my sister fill out her college application when she wanted to give up

☆

THE CARTOON ANIMAL

Since we've now practiced how to focus our attention on our strengths, values, and unique qualities using **The Multifaceted Gemstone** and **Inner Hero,** let's explore some ways to view our perceived flaws from a kinder perspective.

Sometimes, when we think of the things we think are "wrong" with us, there is a tendency to slip right into **extreme thinking,** which instantly sends our inner critic straight into a tizzy. Suddenly, those old negative **self-stories** we were just starting to get better at changing with the **Story Selector** come flying out of our mouths: "I'm so weird!" "I'm so dumb!" "Why can't I do anything right?" "Why am I so awkward?" etc., etc., etc.

In this way, it can sometimes be challenging to look at our perceived flaws with any kind of gentleness, because just as we start to, our inner critic drives our **Self-Talk Meter** all the way down to low. And our moods and feelings about ourselves can sink easily in this way.

So, wouldn't it be great to find a way to think thoughts about the flaws and quirks we may have without setting off this **Self-Talk Meter** tailspin? Wouldn't it be great to lighten up about our perceived flaws instead of treating them with such heaviness and despair?

Name It and Tame It

In *The Ultimate Anxiety Toolkit* I came up with **The Nametag** tool, where I suggested that people draw out their inner critic as a silly cartoon character and give it a ridiculous-sounding name. For many people, this helps them to see their inner critic as something easier to deal with rather than as something intense and scary. For instance, if your inner critic looks like a squeaky squirrel, it's way easier to imagine shooing it aside than if you picture it looking like a gigantic fire-breathing Godzilla.

Drawing on paper can also be very helpful to our brain, as it uses different areas of the brain related to complex reasoning, which can help us process and retain information more effectively (Umejima *et al.* 2021).

Neuroscience nugget: In a study (Bell and Robbins 2007), researchers told participants to list their worries out on paper. Then, they had one group do "free drawing" for 20 minutes while another group simply looked at different works of art. The participants who did "free drawing" experienced a greater reduction in negative mood symptoms than those who didn't draw. Sometimes, drawing things out on paper can help you draw out happier emotions, too!

Find Your Cartoon Animal

After many years of trying to come up with exercises that could help many clients who were struggling to see their own personalities with kindness, I came up with a tool that was similar to **The Nametag**, in that it utilizes drawing and silliness in its approach in order to give us a different perspective on things. It's called **The Cartoon Animal**.

When my kids were really little, we watched a lot of cartoons centered around cute animals (in fact, this seemed to be what most kids' shows were about). There was one show where a tiger, a cat, and a platypus attended school together. Sometimes the cat was bossy, the platypus was shy, and the tiger often messed things up. But, however different they were, or however many mistakes they made, they were always ridiculously cute animals.

If only we could see ourselves in this way!

When we tend to get too "harsh" in our assessment of our own personality, we are typically leaning toward this distorted belief:

Being perfect = Everyone will like me

Not being perfect = Everyone will hate me

In reality, no one is perfect (this we already logically know), and often,
people around us love us for our flaws, our eccentricities, and all the little
things that make us different.

If you don't believe me right now, think about a cute pet for a second.

Our pets are far from perfect.

Your dog is not 100% perfect. Neither is your cat.

Trust me, I know, because I have two cats. They leap up on the kitchen
counter when they're not supposed to. One likes to steal groceries out of
the bag and drag them across the table (and genuinely thinks no one will
see him doing this). My other cat is an avid toy collector and has a stash
of fake mice hidden under the sofa that no one is allowed to touch or he
loses his cool. When anyone rustles a bag, one of my cats gets big and
poofy, and hops sideways like an electrocuted crab.

Do we dislike them for these flaws? On the contrary, we think the cats
are amazing and adorable. We tell so many loving stories about the cute
things the cats do that it comprises the majority of our conversations at
home. If they were 100% perfect, they would be boring by comparison!
The fact that they have unique quirks and qualities doesn't prevent them
from being lovable; it makes them more lovable, in fact.

We can often appreciate and love these little differences, flaws, and
quirks in our pets, so isn't it time we learned to love these things about
ourselves, too? Since it's sometimes easier for us to look at our pets through
a kinder lens than ourselves, let's use this to our advantage with this particular exercise.

A Kinder Lens

If you were an animal character on a cute animated children's show, what would you be?

First, picture what type of **Cartoon Animal** you'd be. Next, think about both your strengths and your flaws from the perspective of a cute penguin, a fuzzy panda, a cuddly koala, etc. For instance, are you a bossy but clever cat with fluffy fur and a big satin bow? Are you a caring and sweet panda who sometimes forgets his lunchbox at home? Are you a floppy-eared bunny who sometimes gets a little stressed out but who also loves to dance and sing?

This exercise just might jar you out of seeing yourself through an overly critical lens, and allow you to see yourself through a kinder lens instead.

You can also use this exercise to see people you interact with in a different way, too. Try drawing out your partner, your friends, your boss, your family, your co-workers as cartoon animals and see if this works to shift your perspective on them a little bit, too.

Before you say that this whole exercise is "silly," ask yourself: "Can I lighten up a little and allow myself to be silly (and not so serious) for a moment?"

Neuroscience nugget: In a study done at Western Carolina University, researchers studied happiness and how it correlated to having a sense of humor. In their findings, they concluded that "happiness positively related to self-enhancing and affiliative humor styles; it related negatively to self-defeating and aggressive humor styles. Thus, happy people habitually engage in positive uses of humor and avoid engaging in negative uses of humor in daily life" (Ford, Lappi, and Holden 2016, p.320).

So, now that we know that sometimes being silly is good for us…how silly can you make your **Cartoon Animal?**

*When we lighten up on how we see ourselves,
we can lean into kindness a little more.*

I challenge you to unleash all that cartoon cuteness out onto paper!

Worksheet: Draw it out!

Draw yourself as a ridiculously cute **Cartoon Animal**. Then, draw out funny personality traits of this animal, write some cute catchphrases the animal might say, and try to see your perceived flaws in a lighter, kinder way through this exercise. If you want, you can also draw out a few people you know as cute cartoon animals, too, and see if it shifts your perspective a little.

CHAPTER ROUND-UP

☑ Use your imagination to delight and inspire you.

☑ Discover the different sides of **The Seesaw** with different subjects.

☑ You are greater than just one thing you do.

☑ Connect with your own **inner heroic** strengths and values.

☑ Learn to see your personality through **a kinder lens**.

☑ Start to tell the story you want to live.

CHAPTER 3

When You Want to Achieve Your Goals...

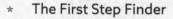

* The First Step Finder
* The Road Block Remover

* The Good Enough Zone
* The Small Wins Book

THE FIRST STEP FINDER

Many of us tend to *overestimate* how much we can do in one day, and *underestimate* how much we can do in an entire year. We have trouble stretching our **time perspective** to see that, over a lengthier period of time, it's possible for us accomplish really big and amazing things if we just keep moving forward a little each week.

Instead, we only want to make huge instant leaps forward, and we want to do this every single day, which puts unrealistic expectations on ourselves, and generally tends to tank our confidence about accomplishing anything.

Neuroscience nugget: Studies have shown that the amygdala (which triggers emotions) and the frontal lobe (which processes information and forms strategies) communicate with each other in different ways depending on how we actually *feel* about the goal. In a recent study, researchers found that if people felt very motivated to achieve their goal, this led them to view the goal as easier to accomplish and less difficult to do (Cole, Balcetis, and Zhang 2013, p.18).

Our brains tend to need some element of fun and some sense of "I can really do this if I try!" to get motivated to move forward.

This is often how we get ourselves stuck. We freak ourselves out with unrealistic expectations, criticize ourselves at the end of the day because we didn't accomplish those unrealistic expectations, and then we feel defeated that we haven't moved forward at all. It's a mental trap we tend to put ourselves in.

Consider that there is an easier way to approach accomplishing goals that can lead you to a happier place emotionally. It simply requires you to practice breaking your goals down into smaller steps that feel easier and more manageable to do consistently each week.

Break Those Big Goals Down

Often, the endpoint of a goal seems like it's sitting all the way at the top of a steep staircase we must climb. When we try to see all the way to the top from the bottom, and when we try to estimate how many stairs we're going to have to climb, it's really easy to get really overwhelmed really fast.

Instead, to reduce our overwhelm, what we need to do is to narrow our focus down to finding the **first step forward**. Imagine the goal path is like a staircase covered in fog. As you move forward, you see another step, then another one, and then the fog clears and you can see the top. You can't always get this perspective looking up from the bottom. You have to start moving up the stairs first to start to get some clarity on what's coming next.

Find the First Step

The First Step Finder can help us do this. To begin with, take any goal you would like to work on accomplishing. Let's try a sample goal to start with:

Sample goal: I would like to get a better job.

Now, set a *realistic* time frame to accomplish this goal in. Usually, when someone's unhappy with their current job, they want to find a new job instantly to relieve them of the stress they're feeling in the moment. We want to avoid this **instant fix** approach when you are goal-setting, as this will only put more pressure and stress on you, which won't make the process feel any easier to navigate.

Ask yourself: "What is a realistic time frame for this to happen?"

Realistic time frame: Six months.

Now, break down this large goal into smaller monthly goal steps. If you want to find a job in six months' time, what will you need to do *each month* until then?

Monthly goal: Send out 8–10 resumes a month.

Now, take that monthly goal and break it down to a weekly goal that sounds manageable to you:

Goal: Find a better job.

Realistic time frame: Six months.

Monthly goal: Send out 8–10 resumes a month.

Weekly goal: Send out 2–4 resumes a week.

We now have a **weekly goal**. Ask yourself, "After looking at my list, what's the **first step forward?**"

Remember, this is the simplest, easiest step you can take to get yourself moving toward your goal. Let's try this:

Goal: Find a better job.

Realistic time frame: Six months.

Monthly goal: Send out 8–10 resumes a month.

Weekly goal: Send out 2–4 resumes a week.

First step forward: Find my old resume on my computer and update it.

Now, there is a clear, small, actionable step that we can take today. We've gone from the overwhelming "Must instantly find a new job!" to "All I have to do is edit my old resume today." Which of these sounds better to you?

Here's another example from a client:

Client's goal: Do more yoga to get in better shape.

Realistic time frame: One year.

Monthly goal: Do complete yoga routine 4–6 times a month.

Weekly goal: 1–2 yoga routines.

First step forward: Buy a new yoga mat.

In this client's case, his first idea of a manageable monthly goal for yoga was initially higher; in fact, he wanted to do one hour of yoga per day. However, after some discussion, he realized that this was a bit too high an expectation to have for himself after a long stressful day of working from home.

I asked him if he wanted to change his weekly goal to "One yoga workout per week" instead.

He paused and then said: "But if I don't do yoga every day, it's not worth doing."

He froze for a second, realizing he had just bumped into a strange belief he hadn't known he had.

"I don't know why I just said that," he laughed, "Because even as I said it, I realized it really wasn't true at all."

We laughed about this, because we've all been there before! Sometimes, we have strange unexamined beliefs about how often or how much we need to do something, and these beliefs are holding us back from moving forward.

"After all, if I do even a little each week, it's still better than me doing none at all," he then added. "If I do a little each week, it's bound to make a difference in a whole year's time, if I think of it that way."

By getting this client to realize that in one year's time he could get to where he wanted to go, he began to feel more motivated to start moving forward in small weekly steps.

The First Step Prep

The **first step prep** is what you do to mentally prepare yourself to do your first step forward. It's like a tiny **mental nudge** that gets you moving forward a little.

In this client's case, after he bought a yoga mat, he kept it in his car because he didn't know where to keep it in the house. When it was time for his weekly "Yoga Workout Day," he was so tired from work that he didn't want to go down to the garage to find the yoga mat in his car. At our next session, he confessed that the yoga mat was still sitting in his car.

So we decided that his first step prep would be to go get the mat, and then, roll it out onto the floor on the morning of his next workout day. This way, at six o'clock, after work was over, he would see the mat in the room, and it would be easier to just get started. When we can visually see our first step prep in front of us (such as a yoga mat rolled out on the floor), it helps prime our brains to take the next step forward.

His new list looked like this:

Goal: Do more yoga to get in shape.

Realistic time frame: One year.

Monthly goal: Do complete yoga routine 4–6 times a month.

Weekly goal: 1–2 yoga routines.

First step forward: Buy a yoga mat.

First step prep: Roll out the yoga mat on the morning of each workout day.

This "roll the mat out" ritual wound up working really well, and he soon discovered he was accomplishing his weekly goal consistently and it was quickly becoming a habit. After a month, he was automatically prepping his mat on the selected day; he no longer had to think about it. The new habit had been completely formed.

The client called it this the "**Go Get the Mat Rule**" and sometimes referred back to this when he started other goals.

"Now, when I get stuck on other goals, I tell myself, 'Just go get the mat!' and then I know what I need to do," he said, in a later session.

Sometimes, you just need to...go get the mat!

The Mental Nudge

What's a **mini-first step** toward your goal? If your goal is something like, "Get out into nature more," maybe your **first step prep** is putting your hiking shoes by the door. For some, the first step prep might be holding their car keys in their hands for a few minutes before deciding to drive somewhere; for others, it might be putting their paint brushes out on a table before they intend to paint something.

Neuroscience nugget: Did you know that when we visualize taking an action, we stimulate our brain's motor cortex? In this way we can "mentally rehearse" doing something and our brain responds as though we are doing it. According to psychiatry professor Dr Srini Pillay, "visualizing movement changes how our brain networks are organized, creating more connections among different regions. It stimulates brain regions involved in rehearsal of movement, such as the putamen located in the forebrain, priming the brain and body for action so that we move more effectively" (Pillay 2015).

Doing something like putting your hiking boots by the door and imagining yourself going hiking prepares your brain to do the task by activating your motor cortex with your imagination.

You can remember it like this:

Do the easiest, tiniest thing to get yourself moving forward.

Even if it just means putting on a pair of shoes, put on the pair of shoes! Know that the motivation will find its way to you as soon you put those shoes on and start heading out the door.

Instead of waiting for a big wave of motivation to take action, take a small action first, and the motivation will follow.

Take the First Step Forward

To review:

1. Break your goal down into manageable monthly goals.
2. Break your monthly goal down into manageable weekly goals.
3. Ask yourself: What is the **first step forward**? And then, write it down.
4. Ask yourself: What is the **first step prep** I need to do? And then, do it before you take your first step.

Small steps really do add up—you just have to find the first one to take.

Worksheet: Write it out!

Let's practice setting your **first step forward** toward a goal you want to work on. Establish a realistic time frame for your goal. Then, break down your monthly goal down into weekly goal steps, and then, figure out what the first step forward will be. Your **first step prep** is a tiny mental nudge to get yourself mentally ready to go! For example:

Goal: Finish painting a small painting.

Realistic time frame: Within three months.

Monthly goal: Finish a section of the painting each month.

Weekly goal: 1–2 hours a week of painting.

First step forward: Prepare and stretch the canvas.

First step prep: Tonight, I will put out my paint brushes on the table to remind myself that it's painting day tomorrow.

Now, it's your turn.

Goal: . . . .

Realistic time frame: . . . .

Monthly goal: . . . .

Weekly goal: . . . .

First step forward: . . . .

First step prep: . . . .

THE ROAD BLOCK REMOVER

We often place hurdles in our way on our path to our goals. We "bury" the yoga mat in the car, we can't find a class to take on the right day so we never take it, we get distracted finding the "perfect" gear that we never purchase, and we do all sorts of things to stop ourselves before we even get started. I call these types of things **mini-road blocks** and we tend to place them in our own way when we're just starting to move toward our goals.

For example, a client wanted to buy a new wall calendar to use to track self-care goals on. Instead, after visiting a few stationary stores and not finding the exact style of calendar she was looking for, she went home and never started her goal-tracking calendar.

"I never found the right calendar I wanted," she confessed, "So I just went home. And then, I never started tracking my goals at all. I stopped myself before I started."

Another client set a goal of using DJ software to make music, but instead, found himself stuck at the starting line, trying to find the "perfect" pair of headphones to purchase before he could begin.

"Every week, I keep searching for the right pair of headphones, then I get anxious and feel like I'm going to pick the wrong ones, so I don't buy any. I can't move forward making music, because I haven't found the right headphones yet. But I won't let myself use the old headphones, because they just don't feel right to me," he said in session. "I feel like I'm getting myself stuck here on purpose but I don't know why."

Does this type of problem sound familiar to you?

Mini-road blocks are like frustrating little traffic cones that we've put in our own way to our intended destination. Why do we do this to ourselves just when we're finally getting excited to head toward our goals?

The Goal Path and Why It Scares Us

Maybe, on some level, the goal path ahead still feels too "scary" to start down. Typically, when people break down their goal into an easy, manageable first step, they tend to feel way less afraid of the goal path ahead. But what happens if you're still feeling stuck after you've done all that?

There can be many reasons for fearing the goal path ahead. Some common ones include:

* **No clear intention for doing the goal:** Perhaps you're not really certain why you want to accomplish the goal? Sometimes, it can help to write down your intention for completing your goal in a few simple sentences. What do you want to feel when you complete this goal? Take a few minutes to visualize this feeling and connect with it.

* **Your Self-Talk Meter might be running low:** When we're feeling unmotivated or blocked, it's possible that we might be telling ourselves, "I don't know what I'm doing!" or "I'm awful at finishing things!" When we're doubtful of ourselves, criticizing ourselves, or being overly harsh toward ourselves, we won't feel very motivated to move forward. When you change your self-talk, you also change your motivational levels. Start saying more encouraging, soothing words to yourself, such as, "I can figure this out one step at a time" or "I don't have to know all the answers, I just need to take one small step forward and I will figure it out."

* **A fear of failure:** This happens when we fall back to **extreme thinking** again. This is where you decide that there is *only* success or failure at the end of your goal. When we start thinking of these types of "extremes" it can zap the fun right out of the goal journey altogether. It puts too

much pressure on us to "succeed" before we've even tested the water. Instead, give yourself some room to experiment. Expand your definition of what "success" is to include trying things out, figuring things out as you go, and seeing where the path leads you.

* **A fear of success:** Again, this is the same problem as above, only now your **Negativity Lawyer** has somehow decided that even if you do succeed at your goal, it's going to be some kind of "disaster" anyway. Essentially, you have accidentally created a no-win situation for yourself. Instead, take off the **extreme thinking** glasses so you can see the world from a broader perspective. Tell yourself: "Every time I try something new, I'm learning and growing, and that's a good thing."

* **The "newness factor":** Sometimes, it's simply down to the "newness factor." When something feels new, and outside of our comfort zone, it generally causes us to feel a certain amount of anxiety and stress. Even if it's just playing around on new software, or attending a new class, these things can feel stressful because we've never done them before. But the experience won't feel strange and uncomfortable in this "new" way forever; in fact, it won't even feel that way for very long at all. Accept the feeling, breathe into the feeling, and acknowledge that it will soon pass.

Removing the Road Blocks

Now that you have probably identified some **mini-road blocks** you may have put in your own way, how do you remove them?

Here are some steps that may help:

* **Change your self-talk:** Using **The Self-Talk Meter,** find ways to walk yourself over to the middle or high end of the meter, so that you can encourage and motivate yourself with the words you say to yourself.

* **Figure out an easy workaround:** If you're getting stuck on little details and decisions, figure out a simple workaround to make things easier

on yourself. Move yourself around the road block that's getting in your way. Here are some examples from clients of **road block workarounds**:

"I spent two months trying to find the right organizational app so I could accomplish my goal of getting more organized. I never found the right app! Now, I just use a notebook each night and I keep it by my bed so I can see it. It's working well because it's a lot simpler to do."

"I told myself that in order to become proficient, I had to practice speaking Italian every day. But then I couldn't find anyone to practice with in person, so I stopped studying it altogether. Then, I realized I should just take an online class instead—I signed up for one and loved it—plus I met some people in the class and now I have people to talk to in Italian outside of class."

* **Give yourself a decision deadline:** If you're stuck in a **decision-making loop** (such as picking out the proper gear, apps, software, etc.), before you get started on your goal, give yourself a firm **decision deadline**. Write it on your calendar. Tell yourself, you can go back and forth as many times as you want, but by the selected date, you will make a decision. Sometimes, even setting this decision deadline makes you feel more motivated to start moving.

The next time you catch one springing up in front of you, tell yourself, "That's just a **mini-road block,** I don't have to put that there. It's not helping me get to where I want to be. There's an easier way to navigate this and I'm going to figure out what that is."

One Simple Question

A simple question to ask yourself the next time you find yourself stuck at a mini-road block is:

"Is what I am doing today helping me get to where I want to be tomor-row?"

It can be helpful to remember:

If you want to get to somewhere different tomorrow, it starts with making one tiny decision to do something differently today.

Worksheet: Write it out!

Using this free-writing journaling exercise, think of some **mini-road blocks** you may have put in your own way toward a goal recently. Then, ask yourself this question: "Why am I getting stuck here?" Write out the answer to that question in free-form style and see what you discover. Then, figure out how you might remove the road blocks that you've placed in your own way.

Road block: [Write out your road block here]

. . . .

Question: "Why am I getting stuck at this road block?"

Answer: [Let yourself free-write out an answer to this question]

. . . .

. . . .

. . . .

Workaround: [Now, explore some easy ways you can get around this road block]

. . . .

. . . .

. . . .

THE GOOD ENOUGH ZONE

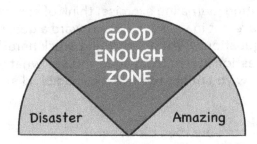

When we're not letting ourselves enjoy the journey toward reaching our goals, it's often because we are putting a lot of pressure on ourselves to be "perfect" or to accomplish something "flawlessly." And then, even *after* we've reached the finish line with goals, we can often become overly critical of our goal completion, telling ourselves it wasn't done "perfectly" or "flawlessly."

It's like being an overly critical and "harsh boss" to yourself. Imagine if you had just worked really hard to complete a challenging task at work and a "harsh boss" came by your desk and said, "Well, this isn't 100% percent, so I won't count this job as being done."

This would sound *really bad* if we heard it coming from another person. In fact, we might even quit! But somehow, when we say these same words to *ourselves*, instead of labeling them as "harsh" or "cruel," we just accept them as "the truth." Have you ever found yourself accepting your own harsh words as "the truth" instead of challenging them just a little?

Neuroscience nugget: Across five separate scientific studies, researchers discovered perfectionism caused a "negative association between self-criticism and goal progress." Throughout their studies, the researchers observed that one key factor of perfectionism was "dispositional self-criticism" (Fleet 2012). Perfectionism, which is often caused by consistent negative self-talk, just might be holding you back from getting your goals.

Next time you get stuck in the **all or nothing thinking** of perfectionism, try using this mental approach instead. If you tend to see "Amazing!" on one end, and "Disaster!" on the other, I'd like you to now picture a very large, sweeping middle area called the **Good Enough Zone**.

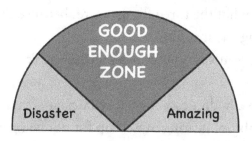

Figuring out what the **Good Enough Zone** feels like to you will help you avoid seeing your performance on tasks and goals through "perfectionist glasses."

The Good Enough Baseline

In order for this tool to work, you first have to understand what the **good enough baseline** is for the task you want to complete. This will help establish a **mental marker** for yourself to help establish what a satisfactory set point is for competing the task. It's there to help you quantify what's essential and what needs to happen.

For example, I had a client who was experiencing a high level of anxiety over a work presentation she had to give. To reduce her anxiety, and to simplify things down, we worked on trying to discover what the good enough baseline was for the presentation.

After some discussion, the client whittled her long list down to these three items:

* I show up on time.
* I give the slideshow I prepared.
* I answer a few questions afterward.

Establishing this good enough baseline was enough to bring this client's anxiety down a few notches, and she started to feel like she might be able to handle the presentation after all. At her next session, I asked her if she had accomplished her good enough baseline list.

"Yes! And it went really well!" she said, "I was so nervous, I was glad we had discussed what the three things were, because that was all I remembered to do during the meeting."

"So, now, can you say you completed the task in the **Good Enough Zone?**" I asked.

"I can! But if we hadn't established what that was, I think I'd be falling back to my old habit of beating myself up for not being perfect. But instead, I'm just happy that I got through it," she admitted.

You can remember it like this:

Simplifying down expectations = Raises confidence

When we simplify things down, we increase our own feelings of being able to complete what we have to do.

How We Zap Our Own Fun

When we make our expectations too harshly unrealistic, and we put so much intense pressure on ourselves to be "perfect," we lose any sense of "fun" along the way. And our brains are always searching for the "fun" in things we have to do, in order to keep our focus, interest, and attention fully engaged.

For example, after using **The First Step Finder**, one client decided she would start to take one beginner dance class a week as a way to "connect with fun things" that she liked to do. She was trying to find ways to destress from her demanding job, and taking a class where she could just move around to music seemed like a good plan. After one class, she felt "really energized and inspired" and wanted to keep going, and so she quickly signed up for additional classes.

However, over the course of the next few months, she started to put a lot of unnecessary pressure on herself. She said: "I found myself getting really competitive in class, telling myself I needed to get better faster, doing too many classes in a row, and the next thing I knew, I was signing up for an intensive dance workshop that was way too advanced for me. And then, all of a sudden, it didn't feel fun anymore, it felt stressful. I think I 'zapped' my own fun!"

Have you ever zapped your own fun in this type of way before?

After some reflection, the client admitted, "There was a point where I was only going twice a week to easier classes and that felt good enough to me. I should have caught myself at that point and I could have enjoyed it more, had more fun, and ramped up more slowly over time. Instead, I overcomplicated things by being so hard on myself and by expecting myself to be at an advanced level from the start."

Tell yourself that it's okay to be in the **Good Enough Zone** with many of the things that you do. In fact, sometimes it's the way to find your way back to fun again.

When You Want to Go Further

This doesn't mean that you can't challenge yourself to do more and achieve more when you want to. If you want to go further with an activity or goal, and that feels fun and inspiring to you, and you're keeping yourself balanced in a healthy way, then go for it!

However, if you're starting to get really off-balance, things aren't feeling fun anymore, and you're feeling burnt-out, it's probably time to reassess things.

Finding the Good Enough Zone

Here are some ways to remember how to find the **Good Enough Zone:**

* List the good enough baseline for completing the task.
* If you accomplish them, tell yourself you made it to the **Good Enough Zone.**
* Add in soothing self-talk afterward, for example:

"I did a good enough job and I'm going to let myself feel proud of myself."

"I am learning to slow down and appreciate what I'm doing more."

"There is no rush, I can go at my own pace. I am figuring things out as I go."

"I am doing enough. I will continue to do enough. I can feel proud of what I'm doing."

Take those "perfectionist glasses" off for a few seconds, and see how your whole perspective suddenly shifts in a positive direction, one that allows you to feel good about things you're doing.

Learn to let yourself feel good enough, more of the time.

Worksheet: Write it out!

Pick a task you want to complete and establish what the good enough baseline is for you, which should be reasonable-sounding "satisfactory set points" required to complete the task. Break it down into three "good enough baseline" items that will let you know that you have reached the Good Enough Zone for this task. For example:

Task: Work presentation at meeting

* I show up on time.
* I give the slideshow I prepared.
* I answer a few questions afterward.

Task: . . . .

Item 1: . . . .

Item 2: . . . .

Item 3: . . . .

Task: . . . .

Item 1: . . . .

Item 2: . . . .

Item 3: . . . .

Write out a few self-talk phrases of encouragement you can tell yourself when you reach the Good Enough Zone with these tasks:

. . . .

. . . .

. . . .

. . . .

THE SMALL WINS BOOK

Now that you're moving toward your goals in small weekly steps, how are you starting to feel? Are you actively letting yourself connect with the progress you're making on things? Are you letting yourself feel happy about all of the forward steps you've been taking?

Unfortunately, most of us don't do this very often. Instead, it's very easy for us to decide we aren't allowed to feel happy unless there's a "big win" as we often feel like small wins are too insignificant to celebrate. When we wait to feel good until milestone goals are reached, we miss out on the opportunity to feel happiness in small bursts along the way.

The problem with this approach is that, often, when you finally accomplish a "big win," it can sometimes be challenging to actually let yourself feel good as a result. Have you ever experienced this? It's like, when we finally get what we want, why don't the happy chemicals get released automatically in our brains and give us a big burst of joy?

Sometimes, it's because when you haven't practiced what you want to feel, feelings like pride, joy, and happiness may not be all that easy for you to access when you finally give yourself some permission to feel them.

Instead, start to allow yourself to feel proud of yourself for the small wins you're accomplishing along the way, and then, you'll be able to easily feel proud of yourself when the big wins start to happen.

One way to start tracking your goal progress and to start feeling prouder of the steps you're taking is to keep a consistent **Small Wins Book** over the course of a few months.

Neuroscience nugget: Dr Gail Matthews had conducted a goal-setting study using 149 participants divided up into different groups with different goal instructions. She found that the group that accomplished their goals at the highest success rate was the group that had to write their goals down, come up with an actionable plan, tell a friend, and then report their goal progress to their friend. When we actively track our own goal progress and find ways to be accountable for our progress, we tend to have a much higher chance of completing our goals (Matthews 2015).

Witness Your Progress

Start to notice the weekly steps you're taking toward your goals by writing them down in a **Small Wins Book** consistently. For example, which of your small goals did you finish this week? What first step did you find, or what **first step prep** did you complete? Did you "go get the mat," so to speak? Write it down in your **Small Wins Book**.

Choose a day on your calendar each week to update your **Small Wins Book**. Before you add new entries for each week, take a few seconds to reread what you've written the week before. As you read what's on the page, give yourself permission to feel proud of yourself, no matter how small the win was.

Progress Bullet Points

A simple way to write out your weekly small wins is to use bullet journaling. Put a bullet mark for each win and write them out in a short list.

For example, if your main goals for the year are related to fixing up your house, your small wins for the week might look like:

* Got quotes from contractor for fixing the roof.
* Cleaned out old clothes and donated to charity shop.
* Picked up paint swatches to compare paints for walls.

Big Wins

When big wins happen, find a visual way to denote them at the bottom of your bullet list. Some people like to use a different color pen or a different bullet symbol. Some clients like to use stickers, or to draw out small illustrations of their big win. Whatever seems fun to you works!

For instance, we could take the last list and add in a few big wins to celebrate:

* Got quotes from contractor on fixing the roof.
* Cleaned out old clothes and donated to charity shop.
* Picked up paint swatches to compare paints for walls.
* FINISHED CLEANING OUT BEDROOM CLOSET
* FINISHED PAINTING HALLWAY

Think of an attention-grabbing way to mark your big wins on the page. When you flip through all your pages later, you can see how the small steps led you to bigger things, mapped out across a stretch of time.

Walk your way over to those big wins, one small win at a time.

Worksheet: Write it out!

Keep track of all the **small wins** this week in a notebook. These are tiny steps you are taking toward your goals each week, and you can keep a running list. When a **big win** happens, notate it in a different way. Then, reread your list once or twice, and practice connecting to feelings of accomplishment:

Small wins this week:

* . . . .

* . . . .

* . . . .

Big win of the week:

* . . . .

CHAPTER ROUND-UP

☑ Break down your big goals into small weekly steps.

☑ Find the easiest **first step forward** toward any goal.

☑ Remove **mini-road blocks** as they start to block your path.

☑ Let yourself feel good enough by finding the **Good Enough Zone.**

☑ Celebrate **small wins** on the way to **big wins.**

☑ Make one tiny decision to do something differently today.

CHAPTER 4

When You Want to Find Your Balance...

* The Do Nothing Zone
* The Phone Time-Out
* The Balance Buoy
* The Time Parameters
* The Body Scan

THE DO NOTHING ZONE

While it can be good for our self-esteem to set and accomplish goals in a healthy way, it can actually be harmful to our brains and bodies if we let ourselves become a **goal robot** that just darts at full speed from one goal to the next, never pausing to take a break.

When you're trying to be constantly productive, and you're not giving yourself a chance to relax in between things, it can be very easy to become stressed-out and burnt-out.

So, how can we stop ourselves from turning into goal robots that never get any downtime?

One way is to use a tool I call **The Do Nothing Zone**. It's a particular block of time that you set aside either daily or weekly to *do nothing* in between all the times where you're doing something. Think of it like a mental resetting break. It should be at least a half hour long, but if you can stretch it out into an hour or two, this can help you find your calm and regulate your emotions even more.

While this might sound super-easy to do, consider this: it means not checking your phone, not going on your computer, not doing side projects, errands, cleaning, chores, etc.

In other words, actually…doing…nothing!

The Art of Doing Nothing

In many other countries, they have commonly used phrases that express the "doing nothingness" of life. For example, in Costa Rica, they use the phrase *pura vida*, and the basic gist of this is to enjoy the "pureness" and "simplicity" of life. In Italy, they say, *dolce vita*, which means "the sweet life," and they take it further with the expression, *dolce far niente*, which translates as "the sweetness of doing nothing."

In the USA, you might say that we lean toward the opposite philosophy, "The Art of Doing Something." Not only do we not have a similar phrase that sums up the "sweetness of doing nothing" here, we also don't *actively* encourage the idea of doing nothing either. In fact, you could say our society encourages *non-stop productivity* instead.

How many people do you know personally who consistently work past regular work hours each week? How often do you catch your friends, partner, or family members checking their work emails late at night just to make sure they "haven't missed something"?

Many people tell me that their work supervisors send them frequent late night and weekend work requests each week, and that the subtext underneath these messages is: "Well, what else would you be doing anyway?"

How about...nothing?

If you find yourself frequently falling into a pattern of non-stop productivity, ask yourself these questions:

* Can I do nothing without making it feel like "work"?
* Can I allow myself to relax without telling myself I'm "lazy" or "unproductive"?
* Can I do nothing for a stretch of time without feeling "guilty" about it?

Take a few days to free-write the answers to these questions in a journal and see if you meet up with any mental resistance to any of them. Then start to look at how you might shift any core beliefs that aren't allowing you to relax on a regular basis.

The Stress Pressure Cooker

It's important to remember that our brains do not function well in a pressure cooker of constant stress. While productivity can be important in our lives to achieve our goals and tasks, constant productivity can be harmful to our bodies and brains.

Considering that stress hormones like cortisol stay in our systems for several hours after onset (Hannibal and Bishop 2014), spending only a few minutes "doing nothing" each day is probably not enough time to fully reset your brain and body. You might want to plan an hour or two for your **Do Nothing Zone** instead.

How Do You Do Nothing?

During your "do nothing" time, it can be helpful to sit outside, to notice plants, colors, and textures, to take in smells and sounds, and to use your senses during this time. Deliberately using your senses is a **grounding technique** for finding the present moment, and it can be helpful to bring your stress levels down a notch.

Meditation can also be a beneficial way to experience "The Art of Doing Nothing." If you're struggling with sitting in silence, doing a short guided meditation for five minutes along with an app or YouTube video can help you get more comfortable with meditating in shorter bursts.

Neuroscience nugget: In a brain imaging study, researchers Gaëlle Desbordes and Dr Benjamin Shapero studied the brains of participants who consistently meditated over the course of two months. The fM-RIs showed that consistent meditation lessened the activity in the amygdala, which stimulates flight or fight responses and has a central role in anxiety responses. This proved true even when the participants had stopped meditating, causing the researchers to conclude that meditation can change the brain (quoted in Powell 2018).

Sometimes people initially resist the idea of meditation because they envision it will involve sitting on an uncomfortable mat for an hour, or because they think it's "too hard" or "too much work." In actuality, meditating can be as easy as taking a conscious deep breath and focusing on the present moment for a brief minute or two.

One way to practice **conscious breathing** is called **Box Breathing**. This is where you practice taking long, deliberate, deep breaths by inhaling for four seconds, holding for four seconds, exhaling for four seconds, and holding for four seconds.

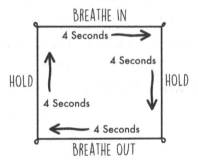

Let Ideas Come to You

The solutions to problems or challenges we have been struggling with may appear when we're finally still and quiet for a moment. You can remember it like this:

Sometimes, you have to stop being busy to stop being stuck.

It can be helpful to let the ideas come to you during downtime, instead of frantically chasing after them during busier times.

Neuroscience nugget: Studies have shown that when we're not focusing on any task or activity, our "imagination network" is activated, which can lead us to new ideas and creativity. According to Jay Dixit from the Neuroleadership Institute, this imagination network "is the brain's resting-state circuitry—the regions that come online when you're not paying attention to anything in particular. This is what activates during downtime" and "the imagination network is central to innovation and creativity" (Dixit 2021).

The Sweetness of Downtime

To avoid becoming a **goal robot** that is always working hard at "The Art of Doing Something," take some time during your day to enjoy the sweetness of "doing nothing." Clear your thoughts and let them slowly drift away. Notice objects, sounds, and colors around you more deliberately. Let thoughts come and go, like passing trains in a station. Take long, deep breaths into the present moment. Sit in your favorite comfy chair, pull up a blanket, and see just how cozy you can feel. Lean into the sweetness of life a little more.

Practice being...

...without doing.

Worksheet: Write it out!

When you think about the **Do Nothing Zone**, what thoughts come to you about what that would feel like? Write out any word associations or sentences that come to mind when you read the phrases below:

"The Art of Doing Nothing" makes me think of:

. . . .

. . . .

. . . .

. . . .

. . . .

"The Sweetness of Life" makes me think of:

. . . .

. . . .

. . . .

. . . .

. . . .

"The Pureness of Life" makes me think of:

. . . .

. . . .

. . . .

. . . .

. . . .

THE PHONE TIME-OUT

We love our phones. I get it. I love my phone, too! I can play any song on it, watch any movie on it, take amazing photos on it, and talk to people all over the world on it. But...let's face it, while our phones may be helping us in many ways, they just might be stressing us out in many ways, too.

I'm talking about **doom-scrolling**, I'm talking about negatively comparing yourself to the social media streams of others, I'm talking about reading depressing stuff on the internet when you should be sleeping, I'm talking about bizarre impulse purchases made out of boredom, I'm talking about getting so distracted by apps that you avoid doing the things you need to do each day. I'm talking about losing hours and hours of time down phone-related **time sinkholes** that, in the end, don't make us feel any better about ourselves.

One client was having trouble completing projects he needed to do because he said he often "got distracted on YouTube for an hour or two here and there." After tracking his app use for a week on a chart, he realized that he was spending 10–12 hours on YouTube each week, and that his estimate of "an hour or two" had been "way, way off."

"I never realized that watching YouTube was causing me so much stress until I stopped doing it," he admitted. "I think I always thought it was bringing my stress down. But it was the opposite. No matter how funny or entertaining the video is, it's not the same as getting out and hanging out with people I like, or working on projects that I want to do. Or even, just letting myself relax a little…without staring at a screen."

We've all been there before! We often think our phones are relaxing us, when in reality they might be draining our mental energy instead.

Neuroscience nugget: A study done at the University of Pennsylvania found that when participants used Snapchat, Facebook and Instagram for over 30 minutes a day, they felt more isolated and depressed than those who didn't use the apps, and when these participants decreased their usage of these apps to under 30 minutes a day, they felt less lonely overall and it generally "improved their sense of wellbeing" (Hunt *et al.* 2018).

Want to improve your sense of wellbeing on a daily basis? Give that phone a daily time-out.

Daily Digital Breaks

For a scheduled time each day, avoid checking your phone texts, apps, and emails for at least an hour. This may sound easy to do, but many people struggle with this at first, because grabbing our phones out of habit has become a very common thing to do.

If you're struggling with setting a regular **Phone Time-Out** for yourself, here are some tricks that might help you remember:

* **Put the phone away at meal times:** When we connect with the food we're eating by focusing on it, we help our brains relax and we aid our digestion. We chew our food slower, allowing us to really taste the food and enjoy it more when we're not distracted. Meals are a natural break in the day and can help your brain to remember to associate "eating" with "no phone time."

* **Leave your phone on a charger in a different room at night:** When you have your phone plugged in on your nightstand, the temptation is to doom-scroll all night long. Instead, try plugging your phone in somewhere a bit farther away and harder to reach, such as the living room or the kitchen.

* **Learn to navigate the uncomfortable FOMO feeling:** Many of my clients tell me they can't get off their phone because of FOMO (Fear of Missing Out). Sometimes, it's a fear of missing important news headlines, but it can also be a fear of missing out on what their friends or colleagues are doing. Sit with the feeling as it arises and breathe into it. It's just a feeling; it will pass.

Here are some self-talk phrases that might work for FOMO:

"I can find out what I need to know in a little while. There's no rush right now."

"Everything will still be waiting for me to look at when I'm done taking some time for myself."

"I don't have to do or be anything right now. I can just sit here and feel peaceful for a while."

Picture how you will feel after spending way too much time on your phone.

Now picture how relaxed you will feel after taking a little break from your phone, after enjoying a few moments of mental space, and not experiencing "information overload" for an hour or two.

The choice is yours: keep scrolling...or give your brain a little break?

Worksheet: Write it out!

Try to identify a few apps and sites that you visit a lot that tend to cause you to feel negative or to experience uncomfortable emotions. Then, log the exact amount of hours you spend on those apps in the log below for one week straight (you can usually find app usage amounts under "Settings" on your phone).

For example:

App/site	Typical emotional response	Hours
Twitter	Stressed out/ depressed	4 hours per week
Phone news feed	Anxious	3 hours per week
TikTok	Sometimes tired after a long stretch	5 hours per week

Now it's your turn:

App/site	Typical emotional response	Hours

☆

THE BALANCE BUOY

As you've made your way through this book, you may be starting to realize that many of the tools are about balance. Whether it's about balancing your **Self-Talk Meter**, your **Seesaw**, your **Self-Stories**, or your **Self-Care** practices, finding your balance helps you find your calm. And finding your calm helps you find your way back to your own amazing inner strength.

In our modern world, it can be really easy to get "off-balance" with things. We overwork ourselves into a state of exhaustion. We people-please too much and forget to take care of our own bodies and brains. We spend so much energy on other people's concerns that we let our own problems pile up until they overwhelm us.

So how can we learn to find our balance again after we've been tipped over for too long?

Finding Your Center

Imagine a buoy in the middle of the ocean. It bobs along in an upright position. If something knocks it over for a second, it eventually resets itself right back to the middle. If it gets tipped over to one side, it quickly recalibrates itself to its upright position.

Your emotional balance is like this buoy. If you tip yourself too far over by doing too much of a certain thing, you might feel emotionally wonky as a result. Maybe this looks like grumpiness, feeling really overwhelmed, short-tempered, stressed-out—it can look different for different people when they reach a level of emotional exhaustion.

When your buoy tips to one side, you would ideally want to note this, acknowledge it, figure out exactly how you got off balance, and then find ways to get yourself back in balance by resetting yourself.

Then your buoy would just bob right back to an upright position and you would feel more centered and grounded again.

Weekly Buoy Check-Ins

Many of us may do this kind of adjusting periodically, but the problem is we don't always do it as often as we should, and we don't do it as *deliberately* enough as we should. Ideally, figuring out how you've gotten off-balance should happen on a weekly basis. But in reality, most of us don't notice how off-balance we are until we've been way off-balance for a really long time, and often when we're already feeling really emotionally wonky as a result.

Instead, consider doing a **weekly Balance Buoy check-in**. When did you tip over too far this week? Did you go too long without sleep? Did you overdo it at work? Did you spend too many hours scrolling on your phone and not getting outside as much as you needed to? Did you stay out too late with friends and now you're feeling grumpy as a result? And what are some ways you can avoid tipping over this far next week? How will you now reset yourself back to the middle again?

Resetting ourselves on a regular basis is one way we can learn to show ourselves more kindness and compassion.

Resetting Yourself

Here are a few examples from clients to see how the **Balance Buoy** works. First, state the situation that "tipped" you over. Then ask yourself some **balance questions** to reset yourself:

Client's example: "I have been working overtime all week and my household tasks are piling up. My dirty laundry is all over the floor, and there are dishes everywhere. I've been eating take-out for every meal and I am starting to feel emotionally drained and really stressed out."

To use this tool, ask yourself these balance questions:

Question: "How did I get off-balance this week?"

Answer: "I had to work too much overtime on a project that I was required to do and I haven't had a day off all week."

Question: "What feels off-balance in this moment?"

Client's answer: "My body hurts. I have been at a desk, eating too much take-out. My house is a mess and it's hard to look at. I feel really stressed out."

Question: "What actions can I take to get myself back in balance?"

Client's answer: "To reset myself, I will take this weekend off. I will spend the weekend at home. Saturday, I will rest my body and make sure I eat a little healthier. It would be good for me to eat some more vegetables or salads over the weekend. Sunday, I will spend time doing laundry, dishes, and organizing things so that my house doesn't stress me out so much."

Question: "What can I do differently in this situation next time?"

Client's answer: "When I have to do overtime next time, I might buy more food ahead of time to have in the fridge so I don't have to rely on fast food. I might make sure to do a little nightly cleanup so it doesn't all pile up on me again. And at night, after I'm done with work, I will do a **Phone Time-Out** so I don't start stressing myself out with work-related stuff all over again."

Let's try another example from another client:

> Client's example: "I had friends stay with me all week and I went out almost every night. On the weekend, we all went to a party. Then I invited more friends over afterward and everyone wound up staying at my house until really late. I had to talk to lots of different people all at once and host them all. I'm feeling drained and a little socially anxious now."

Question: "How did I get off-balance this week?"

Answer: "I scheduled too many social activities during a busy week when I already had people visiting."

Question: "What feels off-balance in this moment?"

Client's answer: "I feel emotionally exhausted, anxious, and I'm getting grumpy about little things."

Question: "What actions can I take to get myself back in balance?"

Then, write out a strategy: "I will take it way slower next week, stay home more, and not do as many social activities. If I go out, I will make sure to not book a bunch of different things on one day. Plus, I'll enjoy going out more if I do it when I have more energy."

Ask yourself: "What can I do differently in this situation next time?"

Client's answer: "I know now that doing two big social events in one weekend plus having overnight guests is too exhausting for me to handle. I think if I have overnight guests, that's enough for one weekend. I will avoid overbooking myself next time."

We all tip our emotional **Balance Buoys** over from time to time. However, when you learn to take deliberate actions to bring your **Balance Buoy** back to the middle more often, you're also learning to regulate your emotions in a healthier way.

Balance Your Buoy

The next time you feel like you've tipped your **Balance Buoy** over emotionally, take a few minutes to fill out the worksheet and ask yourself the balance questions to find your way back to your calm center again.

The more you practice finding your calm center, the more your calm center will start finding you.

Worksheet: Write it out!

Think of the last time you felt like you tipped yourself over, emotionally, by doing too much of one thing (for example, too much work/stressed-out, too much socializing/grumpy). Then, take a few minutes to answer the balance questions below and to think about what actions you can take to bring yourself back into balance.

How did I get off-balance this week?

. . . .

. . . .

. . . .

What feels off-balance in this moment?

. . . .

. . . .

. . . .

What actions can I take to get myself back in balance?

. . . .

. . . .

. . . .

What can I do differently in this situation next time?

. . . .

. . . .

. . . .

THE TIME PARAMETERS

When we're younger, time can often feel endless and we sometimes struggle to fill up our time with things to do. When we start to get older, we begin realize that our time is very valuable, that our time is not actually endless, and then we start to wonder: "Am I spending my time in the way I want to spend it?" and "How can I maximize my time on this planet doing the things I actually want to do?"

This is when it becomes helpful to develop a sense of **Time Parameters**, which involves investigating these two components:

* What are you currently spending your time on?
* What do you *want* to be spending your time on?

By figuring these two things out, and by working on ways to prioritize the things you want to be spending your time on, you will be strengthening your feelings of self-esteem along the way. You'll also be clarifying where you want to go and how you can get there.

Time Priorities

To figure out your **time priorities**, ask yourself, "What are the most important things to me that I want to be spending time on?"

Write out a **Time Priorities Chart** of these things. Then, make a separate **Current Time Chart** and write out the things that you are currently spending time on.

For example, here is an example of a **Time Priorities Chart** and a **Current Time Chart** from a client:

Time Priorities Chart	Current Time Chart
Time spent with my kids and husband at home or out doing things together	Work 9–6 each day
Time to do hobbies I enjoy (photography, gardening)	Time with family 6:30–9 each workday, and weekends when we're not doing other things
Time to relax and unwind at home (not doing work stuff)	Errands 2–4 hours each week
Time to learn new things (languages, new software)	Rushing kids around to play dates and classes, 6 hours a week
Time to travel	Chores 1–2 hours each day, sometimes more on the weekends
	Other social obligations—2–4 hours on some weekends
	Checking emails, text, and off-hours work projects, 4–6 hours per week

Comparing these two lists, the client realized that she wasn't spending as much time as she wanted with her family, she wasn't spending a lot of time relaxing or doing her hobbies, and she definitely wanted to set aside more future time for travel.

"I see where I need to adjust things in my schedule for myself now," she admitted. "It's much easier to see now that it's in front of me like this. I just need to stop more on a regular basis and really think about what it is I really want to be doing instead."

In this way we can direct ourselves to do more of what we want, instead of just doing…by default!

Setting Weekly Time Parameters

Here's one way to visualize setting clearer **Time Parameters** for yourself. **Time Parameters** are little protective barriers you put up around the things you want to do, so that you can actually allow yourself space in your schedule to do them in.

For the sake of this visualization exercise, there are two types of **Time Parameters**, much like lane dividers on a road. There are solid line parameters and dotted line parameters. Like a traffic road, you can cross over the dotted line, but you can't cross over the solid line:

_____

TASK

(solid parameters)

_____

or

. . . .

TASK

(flexible parameters)

. . . .

So, when you're establishing **Time Parameters** around a task, ask yourself: "Is this a dotted line task or a solid line task?" Or is this a solid parameter task or a flexible parameter task?

If the **Time Parameters** around the task are dotted lines, it means they are flexible and open to change or movement. If the **Time Parameters** are solid lines, it means that they are not flexible and they are unmovable. For example, in this client's case, she wanted to mentally mark "time with kids" as a solid line task for Saturdays.

TIME WITH KIDS

(solid parameters)

When you put solid lines around a task, it means you are valuing the importance of that task. You are making it a **time priority**.

Prioritizing Time

After trying out this visualization technique, this client learned not to over-book her Saturdays with too many other social obligations so that she could spend more time with her family. She also learned to put aside time to work on her hobbies on the weekend, instead of just thinking she would do them "at some point" in the "vague future."

"I never realized I could say 'no' to things, because I saw everything as equally important to do," she confessed, "but now I see I have to keep adjusting *which* things are important for me to focus on each week, and I have to make those things more important in my own mind. I also realized

I have to protect my weekends more...except I am honestly just protecting them from myself, because I am the one who tends to overbook things!"

Sometimes, this is *exactly* what we need to learn to do. We need to save our time...from *ourselves*.

Neuroscience nugget: In a large study of 7000 Australians, researchers compared how participants felt about time to how much time they actually had to do tasks each day, and concluded that "those who felt most overworked—those who have least 'free time'—largely do it to themselves" and that "much of the time devoted to paid and unpaid tasks is over and above that which is strictly necessary. In that sense, much of the time pressure that people feel is discretionary and of their own making" (Goodin *et al.* 2004, p.45). So when we say we are "crunched by time," we might actually be the ones crunching our own time!

Chronically Dotted Lines

Where people tend to get into trouble with their **Time Parameters** is when they have too many "dotted line tasks" that aren't fixed or prioritized on their schedules. This typically comes from a habit of "people-pleasing," where we see our own schedules as infinitely adjustable to accommodate the "solid lines" of others.

If your approach to scheduling is to have **chronically dotted lines,** you might move around all the things that are important to you (such as self-care, relaxation, your own creative pursuits, goals, or time with loved ones) to suit the needs and whims of others on a regular basis. Over time, this can create feelings of low self-esteem, because, by rating our own priorities as "last on the list," we're also telling ourselves that we are "last on the list" too.

Sometimes, this comes from our upbringing, from our what our own caregivers modeled to us, or, sometimes it comes from various societal or cultural influences. And sometimes, having flexibility in our schedules is completely necessary. It's just a matter of finding a better balance if you're frequently finding yourself "running out of time" to do what's important to you.

What things would you like to put a solid line **Time Parameter** around to protect a little more in your own schedule?

Worksheet: Write it out!

Make a **Current Time Chart**, listing what you're actually spending your time on each week. Then, write a **Time Priorities Chart**, listing the things you would most like to be spending your time on. Compare and contrast the two lists and see if you can gain any insight about what you would like to prioritize more.

Current Time Chart	Time Priorities Chart
[List things you are currently spending time on and the amount of time each one takes]	[List things you want to be spending your time on in order of importance to you]

☆

THE BODY SCAN

A few years ago, I led a stress reduction workshop for about 30 students and staff at a university. At the end of the workshop, I led a very short guided meditation where I asked people to do a mindful **Body Scan**, where they closed their eyes, took deep breaths, and focused on what they were feeling in their bodies. Then, I asked the group to thank their bodies by simply saying "thank you" inside their minds, at their own pace, and to open their eyes when they were ready.

As I opened my eyes and looked around the room, I was a little surprised to find that a few people were teary-eyed. I asked the group if they wanted to share anything, and one woman confessed, "I just never thought to thank my body before!"

And the man next to her said, "I realized I haven't been very nice to my body lately."

More voices around the room chimed in with things like, "Why don't we appreciate our own bodies more often?" and "Why have I never stopped to think of all the good things my body does for me all the time?"

As we closed out the workshop, everyone in the room seemed to agree that they could benefit from remembering to thank their bodies more often. Months later, I did this same exercise during another workshop for even more participants, and it had almost the same exact result, with people asking the same types of questions afterward, such as: "Why don't I ever notice all the wonderful things my body does for me every day?"

The truth is, as we go throughout our very busy lives, most of us tend to spend a lot of time in our heads, lost in our own thoughts, and it's easy to lose connection with what's happening inside our bodies.

When we finally stop to decompress, breathe, and stay in the present moment for longer than a minute or two, we can finally come back home to our bodies. It's then that we sometimes realize how far away we've drifted away in our minds, and how we may have been avoiding checking in with our bodies for long stretches of time.

Our bodies do so much for us each day. We breathe, we eat, we sleep, we move around, we listen, we talk, we think. We do so many things each and every day—just take a second right now and think of all the amazing things our bodies do that we dismiss as "regular everyday things" but that are really quite extraordinary. Our bodies just keep on going and surviving and keeping us alive, day after day, and that really deserves our respect, awe, and praise.

But instead of praising our bodies for all the wonderful things they do, most of us tend to say harsh, critical, and negative things to our bodies quite frequently instead. We unfairly judge and compare our bodies, hundreds of times each day. We sometimes come down really hard on our bodies if they aren't "100% perfect"! We often don't allow our bodies to reset fully from daily stress, and then, when we don't feel well, we sometimes say negative things to our bodies like, "Why aren't you better yet?!" when we could be saying "Take your time to feel better and rest, thank you so much for all you're doing for me right now."

If we have a lot of negative self-talk going on toward our bodies, this can often cause us to feel anxiety, stress, and low self-esteem. Our bodies tend to need praise, encouragement, soothing, and motivating words, to feel better, to perform better, and to stay calmer.

However, no matter what you've been saying to your body in the past, you can now start to actively change your self-talk toward your body in tiny ways, by leaning into appreciation more in your words and thoughts.

Neuroscience nugget: Across many different studies, neuroscientists have shown that "practicing mindfulness affects brain areas related to perception, body awareness, pain tolerance, emotion regulation, introspection, complex thinking and a sense of self" (Congleton, Holzel, and Lazar 2015). One easy way to practice mindfulness is to check in with your body more throughout the day.

As you do everyday activities, begin to notice and to appreciate all the little things your body is doing for you a little more. When you finish a walk, perhaps you can tell your body what a great job it did. When you take a deep breath, maybe you can thank your lungs for being so strong. When you lie down to sleep, maybe you can thank your body for getting you through yet another day. It starts with these little, tiny daily thoughts that you can start to think, that will, over time, gradually grow into a bigger sense of overall appreciation.

And as you start to feel appreciation, you give your brain a boost of the love hormone oxytocin, which can help us feel calmer and more relaxed.

Neuroscience nugget: When we're stressed out, our amygdala can stimulate the release of stress hormones cortisol and adrenaline. When we feel love, appreciation, or empathy, oxytocin is released, which has "soothing effects" that are "hypothesised to be associated by its stimulation of the nucleus accumbens and the amygdala resulting in dopamine and serotonin release." Studies have shown that feeling **self-compassion** also activates the *self-soothing system* in the prefrontal cortex, which makes us feel more secure and safe (Hannes 2021).

Give your body the little boosts of love and appreciation that it deserves, so it can keep on moving you through the things you need to do.

Scanning the Body

Here's how to do a very simple daily **Body Scan,** where you connect to what's going on inside of your body more regularly:

1. Take a few minutes when you have nothing to do except sit in a cozy chair or lie down somewhere comfortable and quiet without distractions.
2. Close your eyes. Take a few long deep breaths in and out.
3. As you breathe, mentally scan your body, starting with the top of your head. Imagine a pure bright energy going from the top of your head, and working its way down through your body, your shoulders, your torso, your legs, down your feet, and then, slowly, out into the ground.
4. As you do this scan, practice saying "Thank you" mentally, to your body, as you move the energy from your head down toward your feet. You can say "thank you" as many times as you want to, to any parts of your body that you want to, as you move the energy from head to toe.
5. At the end, you can close off the exercise, by adding, "Thank you, body, for everything you do for me every day."
6. When you're done thanking your body, take a long, slow deep breath and slowly open your eyes.

When you deliberately bring your mind back home to your body, you can connect to your powerful inner strength once again.

Worksheet: Write it out!

Think of all the amazing things your body does for you each day. Now, in the space below, write your body a "thank you" letter, thanking it for all the little, tiny, daily things it does for you:

Dear Body,

Thank you for...

. . . .

. . . .

. . . .

. . . .

. . . .

. . . .

. . . .

. . . .

. . . .

. . . .

. . . .

. . . .

. . . .

. . . .

CHAPTER ROUND-UP

☑ Enjoy the sweetness of **doing nothing** sometimes.

☑ Give your brain a break with a daily **Phone Time-Out**.

☑ Stay balanced with a weekly **Balance Buoy** check-in.

☑ Learn to value your time by establishing **Time Parameters**.

☑ Thank your body for all the things it does for you every day.

CHAPTER 5

When You Want to Feel Happier...

* The Reframing Wand
* The Compliment Basket
* The Change Surfboard
* The Mini-Happiness Net
* The Future Picture
* The What's Working List

THE REFRAMING WAND

Here's a tool that can really help you practice more mental flexibility on a daily basis. I call it **The Reframing Wand.**

Many therapists (especially cognitive behavioral ones) tend to use **cognitive reframing** a lot with clients, as well as in their everyday lives. I have often witnessed a group of therapist friends having a casual conversation and watched how effortlessly they cognitively reframe things for each other, back and forth, without even skipping a beat. However, you don't have to be a trained therapist to develop this coping skill that can help you navigate many of life's challenges. You can practice by reframing one tiny thought at a time.

Imagine a magical wand that, when you give it whoosh, it helps you maintain your emotional balance. This is what we're doing when we're mentally reframing a situation—we are actively looking to find something positive or beneficial to zoom in our attention on. We are taking negative thoughts we're having and spinning them around in the moment, so that those thoughts now become helpful, instead of hindering.

A cognitive reframe of a negative statement, such as, "I'll never be able to figure out what to focus on next!" can look like, "I've prioritized tasks before, and I'll prioritize them again," or "Over time, I will be able to figure this out a little bit at a time."

When a disappointing situation arises, such as receiving a job application rejection email, a cognitive reframe might be, "At least now I can sharpen my focus more on getting a position that I really want," or "I am glad I have more time to fine-tune my resume before I submit it again." If a friend cancels at the last minute, a cognitive reframe might be, "Even though I was looking forward to getting lunch, at least I now have an extra hour to read the book I've been trying to finish."

Here's what a powerful cognitive reframe looks like:

When asked by a reporter, "How did it feel to fail 1000 times at inventing the light bulb?" Thomas Edison replied, "I didn't fail 1000 times. The light bulb was an invention with 1000 steps." (Watkins 2019)

You, too, can learn to be skilled in the art of the cognitive reframe.

Neuroscience nugget: Practicing looking at things from different per-spectives can improve our cognitive flexibility, which helps us regulate our emotional reactions. According to neuroscientists from Duke University, "Cognitive behavioral therapy, which teaches individuals how to re-think negative situations, has been shown to boost activ-ity in the dorsolateral prefrontal cortex." The study suggests "that increased activity in the dorsolateral prefrontal cortex may enable people to think about complex emotional situations in different ways, facilitating flexible emotion regulation strategies" (APS 2016).

When Doom and Gloom Set In

Some people compare cognitive reframing to "finding a silver lining" in things. Personally, I think it's about finding a way to stay grounded by turning around thoughts that are going to knock you off course emotionally.

Think of it like a magic wand you can wave to change your own mood.

When the doom and gloom clouds of extreme thinking hover above you, you can pick up your cognitive **Reframing Wand** and whoosh them away, before the emotional downpour begins.

For example, let's say you threw a party and it didn't go as planned, and the **extreme thought** clouds are starting to form overhead: "It's all disaster!" "This was the worst party ever!" or "Everyone hates me and that's why they didn't come."

Now, pick up your cognitive **Reframing Wand** and whoosh them away by asking yourself logical questions:

* Is this thought helping me or not helping me right now?
* What are some ways I can quickly turn this thought around?

How to Activate the Reframing Wand

Here are two helpful statements that can help activate your **Reframing Wand:**

* **"Even though..."** statements: Start a sentence with "Even though." Then state the negative, and then the positive. For example: "Even though my party didn't go as planned, at least the food was delicious and I can enjoy the leftovers tomorrow for lunch," or "Even though a few friends couldn't make it, at least they called to apologize and we can meet up later."
* **"Yes, but..."** statements: Start with "Yes," acknowledge the negative, and then pivot your thought after the "but" with a positive statement. For example: "Yes, it rained on my way to work and I got soaked, but later I enjoyed watching the rain from inside my warm office," or "Yes, my friend was really late meeting me, but it gave me time to return a few phone calls, so I didn't really notice how much time had passed."

And suddenly, just by using your **Reframing Wand** and pivoting a few thoughts around, you can whisk those gloomy emotions away.

Practice a little with easier subjects, and build up to the harder subjects as you go.

Go on and give that **Reframing Wand** a whoosh!

Worksheet: Write it out!

Pick a situation that was disappointing in some way. Using "Even though..."
or "Yes, but..." statements, try to "reframe" the situation a few times, until
you feel a little better emotionally.

Situation:

. . . .

Reframe 1:

. . . .

. . . .

Reframe 2:

. . . .

. . . .

Reframe 3:

. . . .

. . . .

THE COMPLIMENT BASKET

Now that you're getting the hang of achieving your own personal goals, treating yourself with more kindness, and getting yourself back in balance, you might just start to hear a few compliments, encouragement, and praise from other people, too. This seems like it would be a good thing. However…

Often, we do not know how to receive compliments, encouragement, or praise.

When someone says something nice to you, do you wince, blurt out an awkward reply, or swat the compliment away like it's a pesky fly that's trying to land on you? You're not alone. Many people do this.

Even though we really desire praise and positive feedback, when we finally get it, we sometimes have trouble *accepting* the very thing that we wanted.

For people who experience this chronic problem of accepting compliments, it might be that their negative self-talk has become so pervasive and consistent, that when someone says a positive, encouraging phrase to them, their brain instantly wants to reject it. You can remember it like this:

The more you talk to yourself in a kind way,
the more you will accept
kind words from other people.

This also means...

The more you talk to yourself in a harsh way,
the more you will accept
harsh words from other people.

When we're used to telling ourselves kind, encouraging words, and some-one says something similarly kind and encouraging to what we're already telling ourselves, we will hear it, and it will resonate with us more.

If we are constantly criticizing ourselves, and someone criticizes us, we tend to *only* hear the criticism. That's just what we've trained our brains to hear.

Neuroscience nugget: Researchers from the UK NHS Mental Health Foundation studied emotional reactions in study participants after having them imagine a positive social memory. They found that "individuals who are more self-critical find it harder to self-soothe when receiving compassionate imagery," and "are more resistant to positive emotions associated with compassion, and find it more difficult to receive compassionate emotions" (Holden *et al.* 2016, p.57).

In other words, if your self-talk is frequently at the low end of the **Self-Talk Meter,** you might have trouble *hearing* praise and compliments, as well as *receiving* compassion from others.

When you change your self-talk,
you change what you're allowing yourself
to receive from others, too.

Once you fully accept this concept, that *we tend to hear what we're used to telling ourselves*, it can really change the way you talk to yourself on a daily basis.

Using the Compliment Basket

Imagine a **Compliment Basket**. This is a holding place for the compliments you receive. Instead of cherishing and appreciating the compliments in the basket, do you actively dump them out?

A client had received an award and was getting a lot of praise at work.

"You did a great job on that project!" someone said to her.

"No, I really didn't, there were a lot of things that went wrong," she argued. "I have no idea why they gave me that award. I don't deserve it. I didn't even do a great job at all."

So, instead of simply accepting the compliments, she had a knee-jerk reaction to swat all the compliments away! Which is the opposite of what she really wanted to do, which was to emotionally connect with the compliments.

Cognitive behavioral therapists refer to this as **"disqualifying the positive."** Instead of accepting something positive someone is saying, you disqualify it and reject it as invalid. In doing this, you're replacing a positive compliment with your own negative self-talk instead.

"Oh, they're just saying that to be nice," you might say after receiving a compliment when you have "disqualifying the positive" thinking going on. "They're not really giving me a compliment because they think I deserve one."

Some of this **compliment swatting** might come from our upbringing. Many of us were raised to be more sensitive to accepting compliments because it might "make other people feel bad." Perhaps we watched all the adults around us disqualify the positive after something nice was said to them in an attempt to "be humble" or "not look conceited." We may have learned by example that "compliments are awkward" and make us feel really "uncomfortable."

If this is resonating with you in some way, it can be helpful to explore these ideas that might have formed, and ask yourself, "Do I really want to continue holding on to these beliefs?" and also, "How might these beliefs be affecting my self-esteem?"

Accepting Compliments

After working with many clients over the years who had chronic problems accepting compliments, I developed a few simple steps that can help:

1. The next time you receive a genuine compliment, count to three in your head. Sit with whatever you're feeling for three seconds and breathe into it. The three seconds of silence will feel like ten years to you at first. To the other person, they probably won't even notice the three seconds at all.
2. Then simply say, "Thank you."
3. After you say "Thank you," resist the urge to instantly **negate the compliment**. This is usually what people want to do. The urge will be to say something along the lines of, "Oh, it was nothing," or "I really didn't do all that much." Avoid the **knee-jerk compliment negators** if you can. If it feels uncomfortable, that's just because it's a new feeling. Sit with the feeling. Breathe into it.
4. Then, if you are able to, give the person a genuine compliment back. Keep the positive communication going. This will increase the good feelings all around for everyone. See it as kindness being passed back and forth.

By remembering these steps, you can emotionally connect with the compliments you receive and enjoy them a little more.

Compliment Boosters

You can also fill up your own **Compliment Basket** by giving yourself some complimentary self-talk boosters.

If someone says "Great job on that project!" pause and thank them, and then add a mental **compliment booster** to think to yourself: "I worked very hard on that project. I'm proud of myself for finishing it."

If someone says "I enjoyed hearing what you had to say" add a mental **compliment booster** to yourself: "I'm getting better at speaking clearly. It's a good skill for me to keep working on."

If someone says "You really handled that well" add a mental **compliment booster** to yourself: "Every year, I am getting better at handling new situations. I'm learning and growing all the time."

These self-talk boosters work best when they are kind thoughts you're thinking that actively affirm what the person is saying to you.

Compliment boosters help us stretch out the moment just a little bit longer, instead of shrinking the moment by actively swatting it away.

Show yourself some kindness by letting yourself stay inside the positive moments a little longer.

Worksheet: Write it out!

In order to let your **Compliment Basket** fill up, and to not actively "dump it out," let's practice receiving a few compliments on this worksheet! Write down the last three compliments you received, how you reacted vs. how you want to react in the future, and then add a **compliment booster** to say to yourself.

Compliment I received: . . . .

How I reacted: . . . .

How I want to react next time: . . . .

Compliment boosters I can tell myself: . . . .

. . . .

Compliment I received: . . . .

How I reacted: . . . .

How I want to react next time: . . . .

Compliment boosters I can tell myself: . . . .

. . . .

Compliment I received: . . . .

How I reacted: . . . .

How I want to react next time: . . . .

Compliment boosters I can tell myself: . . . .

. . . .

THE CHANGE SURFBOARD

Now that you've made it this far into the book, you're hopefully starting to experience some new positive changes in your thinking patterns and in your feelings toward yourself.

Although change can be beneficial, it can sometimes cause anxiety, because it involves new things that we haven't yet learned to navigate. And new things tend to shake us up a little, even if, in the end, they're allowing us to grow in a more positive direction.

It can be helpful to keep in mind that it's natural to feel a little uncomfortable when you're adjusting thinking patterns you've held on to for years. If you're feeling uncomfortable setting new time parameters, changing your thinking patterns, forming new self-care habits, or telling new stories about yourself, you can begin to see it all as part of the growth process. It's helpful to remember:

The more you practice new ways of thinking, the less uncomfortable they feel.

If you can gently navigate the "uncomfortable feelings of change," you will eventually get to a place where going back to your old negative thought patterns and stories now feels more uncomfortable to you. You may even think, "I don't like the way these harsh thoughts make me feel. How did I ever think these things so frequently before?"

Now, your new "normal set point" is being a whole lot kinder to yourself, so when you experience a setback toward "old" types of harsher thoughts or patterns, they will feel really "off" to you.

See this all as welcome progress. You're shifting things for yourself, a little bit at a time.

Neuroscience nugget: Researchers at the Center for Outcomes Research and Evaluation found that "people have a propensity to simulate negative outcomes, which result in a propensity toward negative affective responses to uncertainty." In other words, because we tend to picture negative outcomes to things, it's easy for us to imagine that change will lead to negative outcomes (Anderson *et al.* 2019, p.1).

It can be helpful to remember that change can also lead to good outcomes, too!

Ride the Wave

Life is full of things that are constantly changing on us—our bodies, our thoughts, our emotions, our perceptions, our circumstances, our stuff, our environments, our responsibilities. And change can make us feel uncomfortable as we're experiencing these shifts happen. So how can we learn to get more comfortable with being uncomfortable?

To ride out the "uncomfortable feelings of change," imagine a magical **Change Surfboard** that will carry to you to calmer shores. Just like an ocean wave, the uncomfortable feeling wave has a crest, which is the point where it feels the most intense to experience. However, you can breathe your way through this swell, and, after a few moments, find yourself gliding along in a smoother way.

When you start to feel uncomfortable with all the new things that are happening to you or in your life:

1. Take a few long, deep breaths. Say inside your mind, "Breathing in... breathing out..." as you breathe.
2. Relax into the feeling; don't fight it. Go into the feeling by breathing into it. Remind yourself: it's just a wave of temporary emotion and you can simply breathe your way through it until you get to the end.
3. Breathe. Focus on breathing. Ride...the...feeling...out...with...each... deep...breath.

You will soon find that the emotion and the moment pass. Let it go with one long exhale.

After the wave of change passes, add in some motivational self-talk:

"I am trying new things, I am learning and growing."

"This is only a temporary feeling. All feelings are temporary."

"New things can be uncomfortable at first but this feeling will pass."

"When something is no longer new, it will no longer feel uncomfortable to me."

"It takes courage to try new things and I'm proud of myself for taking this new step."

By doing these things, you will find that the "uncomfortable feelings of change" will soon pass, sometimes in only a matter of minutes. And then you'll realize that by riding out those feelings of change, you are growing in the process. You are tapping into your inner strength, resolve, and determination a little more.

You can now ride out the wave to much more enjoyable shores.

Worksheet: Draw it out!

Learn to get more comfortable with the "uncomfortable feelings of change" by writing out a few soothing and motivational phrases about change you can tell yourself as you ride out the feeling:

. . . .

. . . .

. . . .

. . . .

. . . .

. . . .

. . . .

. . . .

THE MINI-HAPPINESS NET

Just like when we try to shrink our whole entire human identity into one box, when we try to shrink our definition of "happiness" into one single box, it typically doesn't work out so well for us, emotionally.

For instance, you may be unconsciously "putting off being happy" until "something very specific happens in the future." You may have an unexamined belief that "When I finally make $200,000 a year, I will be happy" or "When I finally get married, I will be happy" or "When I finally become famous, I will be happy" or "When I finally move to a new city, I will be happy."

This would be great, if you felt happy when these things happened to you, and you also let yourself feel happy for many other things along the way, too. But often what happens is because we have pinned our entire idea of happiness onto just one thing, we don't allow ourselves to feel happy until we've obtained that *one* thing. And, as we've learned from **The Multifaceted Gemstone**, this is just way too much pressure to place onto just one thing and onto yourself. Because if that one thing takes a little while to happen, you're setting yourself up to feel instantly unhappy! You can think of it like this:

Distorted belief:

One thing = Happiness

Not getting that one thing right away = Unhappiness

There's also another unexamined belief going on in these distorted equations, which is that "happiness" is a permanent state of being that you will somehow reach by gaining a "thing." In actuality, like all emotions, happiness is just a temporary state of the brain that comes and goes quite frequently, each and every day.

However, if we want to experience happier emotions more of the time, we have to cultivate and practice happier emotions more deliberately and more consistently.

You can now form a new mental equation that will connect you to happier feelings more often:

$$\text{Tiny daily things} = \text{Happy moments to experience}$$

And...

$$\text{Tiny happy moments} = \text{Happiness}$$

Neuroscience nugget: Psychologist and author Rick Hanson summarizes the tendency to look toward the negative as, "The brain is like Velcro for negative experiences but Teflon for positive experiences." He suggests that we direct our attention to positive feelings and stay in those moments more, "That's how we give those neurons lots and lots of time to fire together so they start wiring together. So, rather than noticing it and feeling good for a couple of seconds, stay with it. Relish it, enjoy it, for 10, 20, or 30 seconds, so it really starts developing neural structure" (quoted in Bergeisen 2010).

In other words, observe those **mini-happy moments**, label those mini-happy moments, savor those mini-happy moments, and you will train your brain to really feel the happy moments more as they happen to you.

Find the Mini-Happy Moments

To use **The Mini-Happiness Net,** you might have to make some minor adjustments to how you may currently be defining the idea of "happiness":

* Happiness can happen in small moments throughout the day.
* Happiness can feel like many different types of things.
* Broaden your idea of what happiness is and notice it as it happens in smaller daily bursts and in different flavors.
* Label it as it's happening, even if it's only for a few seconds.

Happiness can come in tiny moments throughout the day and can feel like different versions of happiness. For example, in the morning, you try a wonderful new type of coffee, and that first sip is really delicious and you really enjoy it. And then your phone buzzes and you're off and running to the next emotion. The moment has passed. But for that first sip, perhaps this was what you might start to label "happiness" or "joy."

Later, in the afternoon, you stop to pet a cute puppy you see on the street; it looks up at you with a silly expression that makes you smile. Then, a few minutes later, you've gone into a store, and suddenly, you're browsing aisles, making decisions, and the puppy moment has passed. However, for that brief minute you spent with the cute puppy, you might call this "happiness" or "delightful."

That afternoon, after a long day of work, you sit down in your favorite chair, which feels so comfortable to you. You put on your favorite upbeat song, and you tap your foot along to the music. You feel calm and relieved the day is now officially over. You stretch and let out a long exhale. You might label this deep breath of relief "happiness" or "relaxation."

You don't have to wait for big dramatic moments in life to connect with happy feelings along the way. They can look and feel like all of these tinier types of everyday things, too.

The Different Flavors of Happy

Happiness is happening every day; it is happening to us in tiny, small bursts, and it can take on different types of "flavors." Some of these flavors may be fun, some may be sweet, some may be relaxing, some may be exciting, some may be calming, some may be delightful. What are some other word associations that "happiness" can have for you?

How can you expand your definition of what "happiness" is to encompass a larger range of other types of feelings?

Here are some words that might help expand your definition of "happiness" a little. Circle the ones that stand out the most to you:

Enjoyable	Magical	Humorous
Relaxing	Exciting	Enchanting
Fun	Silly	Adorable
Giddy	Sweet	Funny
Gleeful	Playful	Delightful
Soothing	Inspiring	Delicious
Joyful	Appreciative	Engaging

When you read this list of words, you can probably start to see how they make you feel. Each one is different, but each one can also mean happiness, if you want it to. Pick a few that resonate with you in a positive way and add in some of your own, too.

Catching Happiness

Using **The Mini-Happiness Net,** start to notice when you're feeling these different flavors of happiness in little bursts throughout the day. Now imagine that you're actively collecting these **mini-happy moments** with an imaginary net as they appear:

As you notice a feeling you've now associated with the word, "happy," label the feeling as "happy" in your mind. Say something to yourself like, "This is happy," or "This is a happy feeling," or simply, "Happy feeling." If you want to, you can try the word "joyful," too.

To really savor these feelings a little longer, you can also keep a simple list of all the times during the day that you felt these mini-happy moments.

For example, your list could look like:

* Had a delicious cup of coffee.
* Played with an adorable puppy.
* Watched a new episode of my favorite TV show, which made me happy.
* Had a really funny conversation with my friend that made me laugh a lot.

By writing out your daily list, and then reading it back to yourself, you are practicing the feeling you want to feel.

When you practice happiness in small doses,
you will be able to feel it in larger doses later.

Daily Moments Add Up

Each morning, you have a chance to find a few tiny moments of happiness throughout your day. See how many **mini-happy moments** you can collect this week.

The more mini-happy moments you catch, the more they may start to appear!

Worksheet: Write it out!

Learn to expand your definition of what "happiness" can mean and all the different "flavors" of it that you can feel. Try to list out 10–20 related words (for example, giddy, playful, delightful, fun, etc.):

Words I can now associate with "happiness":

. . . .

. . . .

. . . .

Then, start to collect those **mini-happy moments** more as they happen to you this week. Aim to write down 10–15 per week:

1. . . . .

2. . . . .

3. . . . .

4. . . . .

5. . . . .

6. . . . .

7. . . . .

8. . . . .

9. . . . .

10. . . . .

11. . . . .

12. . . . .

13. . . . .

14. . . . .

15. . . . .

☆

THE FUTURE PICTURE

When I ask clients to tell me where they want to be in a year's time, they will often list a lot of specific details about the location they see themselves in, the place they're living in, and all of the activities that they see themselves doing. For example, they might tell me something like, "I see myself living right near the beach, going swimming in the ocean all the time, and finding a job that allows me to work remotely so I can travel as much as I'd like to."

This is a great place to start with visualizing a happy **Future Picture** for yourself. However, what's missing from this picture? How you are *feeling* when you're doing all these wonderful things. And if you think about it, isn't that a really important piece of the picture? Often, we're not seeking connecting with things as much as we are seeking connecting with feelings.

And that's what we can practice more. Because, when you practice the feelings you want to feel, you can feel them later on when you get to that beach, swimming in the ocean, living that amazing life that you see yourself living.

Tell your brain what you want to feel in the future, and your brain can help get you there.

Start to get really clear about the *feelings* you want to be feeling in the future, and you can start to navigate yourself to your desired emotional destination.

Neuroscience nugget: Researchers at York University had participants practice visualizing "a future scene where current issues were resolved," and then instructed participants to imagine giving themselves "advice on how to get there." This resulted in "significant increases in happiness observable at 6 months and significant decreases in depression sustained up to 3 months." Participants who had been high on the self-criticism scale at the start of the study became "happier in only one week's time" after doing this visualization on a regular basis (Shapira and Mongrain 2010, pp.377, 378).

To get yourself connecting with those positive future emotions in the present moment more, imagine this **Future Picture** you've painted as frequently as possible throughout your day. Maybe while you're waiting somewhere you can start to daydream a little and drift off into your **Future Picture**. Or perhaps at night, when you have some spare time, journal about your **Future Picture** in more detail. Fill out the parts that feel really fun for you to write about.

When you're picturing this future image, savor and relish the good future feelings as much as you can. In this way, we're training our brains to walk into our **Future Picture**, one little step at a time.

Pick Up the Imaginary Paint Brush

Pick up your imaginary paint brush and begin painting your future. Sketch out where you are, what you are doing, and then color it in with future emotions you would like to feel in this future scenario. Are you happy, joyful, relaxed, delighted, excited? What other feelings might you want to add in?

Pick out some colorful feelings and start painting a vibrant **Future Picture** ahead.

Worksheet: Draw it out!

Focusing in on what you want to feel in the future, paint a **Future Picture** of where you want to be in one year's time by filling out the questions below.

Where do I see myself in one year's time?

. . . .

What am I doing in this picture?

. . . .

What am I feeling in this picture?

. . . .

Now, using these ideas, draw a **Future Picture** image in the frame below:

THE WHAT'S WORKING LIST

To close out this book, I wanted to give you a motivating tool that will help you really zoom in your attention on everything in your life that's working out for you already.

It's called **The What's Working List.**

We spend so much time zooming in on things that aren't working out for us throughout everyday life. A dozen things can go *right* for us in a day, and we will focus in on the one tiny thing that went *wrong*. We're often wired this way toward a **negativity bias,** which means we tend to **disqualify the positive** and **maximize the negative.**

Let's tip the balance now by intentionally directing our attention toward what is working out for us, right here and now. Let's mix things up a little by **maximizing the positive** instead.

To begin, actively look at and notice the things that are working out right now, and then write those things down in one journal, every week.

Maybe it's tiny happy moments you caught with your **Mini-Happiness Net,** small weekly ways you've reset your **Balance Buoy,** maybe it's the tiny motivational thoughts that moved you to the high end of your **Self-Talk Meter,** perhaps it's creativity you discovered in your **Inspiration Book, Inner Hero** values that you reconnected with, solid line **Time Parameters** you made for yourself, or motivation you found taking the **First Step Forward.** Maybe it's compliments you collected in your **Compliment Basket,** maybe it's a few **Small Wins** from the week, maybe it's a masterful reframe you made with your **Reframing Wand,** maybe it's an inspiring **Future Picture** you painted for yourself.

Any of it—all of it—write it down in a running list of stuff that's working out for you.

Witness What's Working

To begin to use this tool, simply ask yourself, "What's working for me right now?"

And then, start noticing all of the things that are going well for you. They can be anything big or small, daily, weekly, and monthly things. Big changes you made, small shifts in thinking patterns, tiny habits you changed gradually over time—it's all worth witnessing.

Become a witness

to the good things

that are happening in your life.

It's like putting on a pair of magical glasses that allow you to see your life through a lens of love and appreciation:

When you begin to realize that *you* are the one really making things happen in *your own life*, you can start to see yourself with more love and appreciation, too.

Every time you write something down on your **What's Working List**, encourage yourself, cheer yourself on, give yourself a whole lot of praise, because you're doing many things that are moving you forward right now.

Reread your list often. Enjoy your list often. Delight in your list often. Feel proud of your list more often. Practice the feelings you want to feel.

You are covering yourself in kindness, more and more.

You are getting where you want to go, one step at a time.

You've got this.

Keep on going!

CHAPTER ROUND-UP

- ☑ Turn the doom and gloom around with your **Reframing Wand**.

- ☑ When you change your **self-talk**, you change how you hear praise.

- ☑ Learn to ride out the **"uncomfortable feelings of change"** as they arise.

- ☑ Catch those **mini-happy moments** as they appear each day.

- ☑ Practice the feelings you want to feel.

- ☑ Become a witness to **what's working** in your own life.

Resources

Psychotherapist directories in the US

Psychology Today: http://psychologytoday.com

Therapy Den: http://therapyden.com

Psychotherapist directories in the UK

Counselling Directory: www.counselling-directory.org.uk

National Health Service (NHS): www.nhs.uk/service-search/find-a-psychological-therapies-service

Mental health websites

Anxiety & Depression Association of America: https://adaa.org

National Alliance on Mental Illness (NAMI): www.nami.org

Mind (UK): www.mind.org.uk/information-support/helplines

Mental health charities

Brain & Behavior Research Foundation: www.bbrfoundation.org

Recommended reading

David D. Burns (1981) *Feeling Good: The New Mood Therapy*. New York: Penguin Books.

Thich Nhat Hanh (2015) *Mindfulness: How to Relax*. Berkeley, CA: Parallax Press.

Martin E. P. Seligman (1991) *Learned Optimism: How to Change Your Mind and Your Life*. New York: Pocket Books.

Bessel van der Kolk (2014) *Trauma-Based Therapy: The Body Keeps the Score*. New York: Penguin Books.

References

Almendrala, A. (2017) "This is where self-esteem lives in the brain." *HuffPost*, June 16. www.huffpost.com/entry/self-esteem-brain_n_5500501

Anderson, E. C., Carleton, R. N., Diefenbach. M., and Han, P. K. J. (2019) "The relationship between uncertainty and affect." *Frontiers in Psychology*, November 12. www.frontiersin.org/article/10.3389/fpsyg.2019.02504

APS (Association for Psychological Science) (2016) "Mental flexibility may buffer against emotional stress." *Observations*, November 28. www.psychologicalscience.org/publications/observer/obsonline/mental-flexibility-may-buffer-against-emotional-stress.html

Askelund, A. D., Schweizer, S., Goodyer, I. M., and van Harmelan, A. (2019) "Positive memory specificity is associated with reduced vulnerability to depression." *Nature Human Behavior 3*, 265–273.

Aubele, T. and Reynolds, S. (2011) "Happy brain, happy life." *Psychology Today*, August 2. www.psychologytoday.com/us/blog/prime-your-gray-cells/201108/happy-brain-happy-life

Bell, C. E. and Robbins, S. J. (2007) "Effect of art production on negative mood: A randomized, controlled trial." *Art Therapy: Journal of the American Art Therapy Association 24*(2), 71–75. https://files.eric.ed.gov/fulltext/EJ777027.pdf

Bergeisen, M. (2010) "The neuroscience of happiness." *Greater Good Magazine*, September 22. https://greatergood.berkeley.edu/article/item/the_neuroscience_of_happiness

Buckingham, M. and Goodall, A. (2019) "The feedback fallacy." *Harvard Business Review*, March–April. https://hbr.org/2019/03/the-feedback-fallacy

Burns, D. D. (1981) *Feeling Good: The New Mood Therapy*. New York: Penguin Books.

Campbell, J., Moyers, B. D., and Tatge, C. (2012) The Power of Myth: Joseph Campbell with Bill Moyers (Twenty-fifth anniversary edition). Apostrophe S Productions, Inc. and Public Affairs Television Inc., Acorn Media [distributor]. https://billmoyers.com/content/ep-4-joseph-campbell-and-the-power-of-myth-sacrifice-and-bliss-audio

Cole, S., Balcetis, E., and Zhang, S. (2013) "Visual perception and regulatory conflict: Motivation and physiology influence distance perception." *Journal of Experimental Psychology 142*(1), 18–22. https://pubmed.ncbi.nlm.nih.gov/22449101

Congleton, C., Holzel, B., and Lazar, S. (2015) "Mindfulness can literally change your brain." *Harvard Business Review*, January 8. https://hbr.org/2015/01/mindfulness-can-literally-change-your-brain

Dixit, J. (2021) "Science says it's essential to make time to do nothing." *Fast Company*, December 4. www.fastcompany.com/90701856/science-says-its-essential-to-make-time-to-do-nothing-heres-why

Fleet, G. (2012) "The price of perfectionism." *Association for Psychological Science*, February 29. www.psychologicalscience.org/observer/the-price-of-perfectionism

Ford, T. E., Lappi, S. K., and Holden, C. J. (2016) "Personality, humor styles and happiness: Happy people have positive humor styles." *Europe's Journal of Psychology 12*(3), 320–337. https://doi.org/10.5964/ejop.v12i3.1160

Goodin, R. E., Rice, J. M., Bittman, M., and Saunders, P. (2004) "The time pressure illusion: Discretionary time vs. free time." *Social Indicators Research 73*, 43–70. http://jamesmahmudrice.info/Time-Pressure.pdf

Hannes, S. (2021) "How to love yourself with neuroscience." *The Brainstorms*, January 27. https://thebrainstorms.io/how-to-love-your-self-with-neuroscience

Hannibal, K. E. and Bishop, M. D. (2014) "Chronic stress, cortisol dysfunction and pain: A psychoneuroendocrine rationale for stress management in pain rehabilitation." *Journal of the American Physical Therapy Association 94*(12), 1816–1825. doi:10.2522/ptj.20130597

Holden, N., Kelly, J., Welford, M., and Taylor, P. J. (2016) "Emotional response to a therapeutic technique: The social Broad Minded Affective Coping." *The British Psychological Society 90*(1), 55–69. https://bpspsychub.onlinelibrary.wiley.com/doi/full/10.1111/papt.12095

Hunt, M. G., Marx, R., Lipson, C., and Young, J. (2018) "No more FOMO: Limiting social media decreases loneliness and depression." *Journal of Social & Clinical Psychology 37*(10). https://guilfordjournals.com/doi/10.1521/jscp.2018.37.10.751

Kropp, F. (2006) "Values and self-esteem." In M. C. Lees, T. Davis, and G. Gregory (eds) *AP—Asia-Pacific Advances in Consumer Research* (Volume 7, pp.14–18). Sydney: Australia Association for Consumer Research.

Maderer, J. (2017) "Daydreaming is good—It means you are smart." *NeuroscienceNews. com*, October 24. https://neurosciencenews.com/intelligence-daydreaming-7798

Matthews, G. (2015) "Goal research summary." Paper presented at the 9th Annual International Conference of the Psychology Research Unit of Athens Institute for Education and Research (ATINER), Athens, Greece.

Newberg, A. and Waldman, M. (2012) "Why this word is so dangerous to hear." *Psychology Today*, August 1. www.psychologytoday.com/us/blog/words-can-change-your-brain/201208/why-word-is-so-dangerous-say-or-hear

Pillay, S. (2015) "Can visualizing your body doing something help you learn to do it better?" *Scientific American*, May 1. www.scientificamerican.com/article/can-visualizing-your-body-doing-something-help-you-learn-to-do-it-better

Powell, A. (2018) "When science meets mindfulness." *The Harvard Gazette*, April 9. https://news.harvard.edu/gazette/story/2018/04/harvard-researchers-study-how-mindfulness-may-change-the-brain-in-depressed-patients

Raghunathan, R. (2013) "How negative is your mental chatter?" *Psychology Today*, October 10. www.psychologytoday.com/us/blog/sapient-nature/201310/how-negative-is-your-mental-chatter

Ross, S. (2020) "How does stress affect your body?" *The American Institute of Stress*, February 10. www.stress.org/how-does-stress-affect-your-body-the-latest-research-shows-it-can-vary

Shapira, L. B. and Mongrain, M. (2010) "The benefits of self-compassion and optimism exercises for individuals vulnerable to depression." *The Journal of Positive Psychology* 5(5), 377–389. doi:10.1080/17439760.2010.516763

Umejima, K., Ibaraki, T., Yamazaki, T., and Sakai, K. L. (2021) "Paper notebooks vs. mobile devices: Brain activation differences during memory retrieval." *Frontiers in Behavioral Neuroscience 15*. doi:10.3389/fnbeh.2021.634158

Watkins, B. (2019) "Thomas Edison's theorem for success." *CRY Magazine*, March 12. https://medium.com/cry-mag/thomas-edisons-theorem-for-success-b96591bf7dd1

Watson, L. R., Fraser, M., and Ballas, P. (no date) "Can optimism make a difference in your life?" University of Rochester Medical Center. www.urmc.rochester.edu/encyclopedia/content.aspx?ContentTypeID=1&ContentID=4511&gt

About the Author

Risa Williams is a book author, licensed therapist, and time management coach. She is the author of the self-help book series, *Ultimate Toolkits for Psychological Wellbeing*, which includes: *The Ultimate Anxiety Toolkit, The Ultimate Self-Esteem Toolkit*, and *The Ultimate Time Management Toolkit* (JKP Books). She is also the host of *The Motivation Mindset Podcast*, which features practical tips to help people navigate everyday challenges. She's been featured as an expert in *Business Insider, Parade* magazine, *Real Simple, Wired* magazine, and *HuffPost*, and she writes articles for *Breathe* magazine. Visit risawilliams.com or follow @risawilliamstherapy.